THE COUNTY LANDSCAPES

THE LAKELAND LANDSCAPE

THE COUNTY LANDSCAPES

First four titles

THE SURREY LANDSCAPE
THE DEVON LANDSCAPE
THE SUSSEX LANDSCAPE
THE DORSET LANDSCAPE

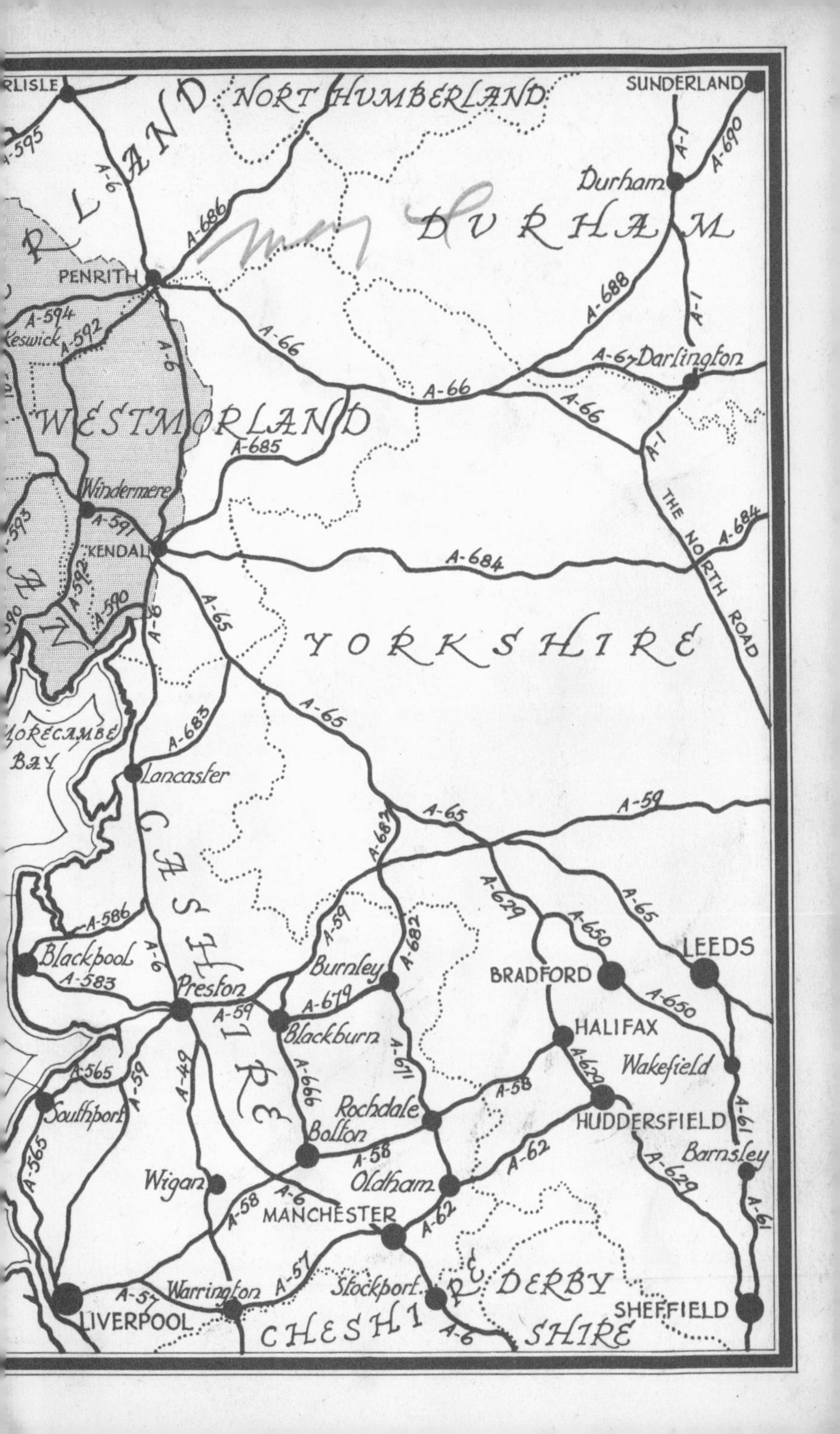

RLISLE
NORTHUMBERLAND
SUNDERLAND
Durham
DURHAM
PENRITH
Keswick
WESTMORLAND
Windermere
KENDAL
Darlington
THE NORTH ROAD
YORKSHIRE
MORECAMBE BAY
Lancaster
LANCASHIRE
Blackpool
Preston
Burnley
Blackburn
BRADFORD
LEEDS
HALIFAX
Wakefield
Southport
Rochdale
Bolton
HUDDERSFIELD
Barnsley
Wigan
Oldham
MANCHESTER
Stockport
DERBYSHIRE
SHEFFIELD
Warrington
LIVERPOOL
CHESHIRE
A-595
A-6
A-686
A-594
A-592
A-66
A-685
A-593
A-591
A-590
A-684
A-65
A-683
A-586
A-583
A-59
A-687
A-629
A-650
A-682
A-679
A-671
A-666
A-565
A-49
A-58
A-62
A-57
A-61
A-1
A-690
A-688
A-67

THE WORKING MEN'S COLLEGE
AUSPICIUM MELIORIS ÆVI MDCCCLIV
Presented By
The Proprietors of
P U N C H.
R.E. Tyler Del. 1913. C.H. Perry Sc.

FRIAR'S CRAG, DERWENTWATER

THE COUNTY LANDSCAPES

THE LAKELAND LANDSCAPE

BY

GEOFFREY CLARK AND

W. HARDING THOMPSON

With landscape map in colour
and sixteen plates from photographs

ADAM AND CHARLES BLACK
4, 5 & 6 SOHO SQUARE, LONDON, W.1
1938

MADE IN GREAT BRITAIN
PRINTED BY MORRISON AND GIBB LTD., LONDON AND EDINBURGH

DEDICATED IN GRATITUDE
TO ALL WHO HAVE WORKED
TO PROTECT THE BEAUTY OF
THE ENGLISH LAKE DISTRICT

INTRODUCTION

In this, the fifth book of the *County Landscapes* series, it has been thought desirable to depart from the method of arrangement previously followed in the studies of Surrey, Sussex, Dorset, and Devon, in which we attempted to portray the individual character of each county as expressed in its physical features. Here, however, Cumberland, Westmorland and Lancashire all contribute to form what is, by nature, a single geographical unit, yet it contains within its imaginary boundary such striking contrasts of scenery as the volcanic mountain masses around Scafell, great stretches of elevated moorland and fell country, and many gentle cultivated valleys on its fringes. There is, moreover, a pronounced similarity in the traditions and characteristics of the old local families who have for so many centuries earned their hard-won living amid the dales and fells, in farming, breeding of Herdwick sheep, quarrying and local crafts. Lancashire, and all that it stands for, seems far removed from the Lake District, even though it possesses much of the shore of Windermere, and the whole of Furness detached from the county by the estuaries and sands of Morecambe Bay; Westmorland has perhaps more completely the characteristics we associate with the Lakes, yet it seems to merge imperceptibly into Yorkshire; Cumberland has its real centre of activity some distance from the region which we here claim as an entity, and as something unique in Britain for its rare beauty contained in so small a compass.

Most of the admirable books written on the Lake

District, since Wordsworth's classic Guide, are confined in their scope to some particular aspect of local life, or to the central area of high fells which is, and always will be, the most attractive to the strenuous walker and climber and to all lovers of romantic scenery. In the following pages we have tried to present an outline picture of the Lake District as a whole, coinciding roughly with the region which has every natural asset to qualify it for protection as a great National Park, and within which local occupations may be maintained and encouraged. To this end a general description of its characteristics may serve a useful purpose, but we cannot do justice to the exquisite scenery in this corner of England without giving a more intimate account of those lovely daleheads which give access to the very heart of the high fells. Each valley and lake has inspired both poet and artist to record its beauty, and each might form the subject of a book. It is indeed with some risk of criticism from those who are well acquainted with every climb and track around Wasdale, Buttermere, and Langdale, that we have chosen to sketch so briefly the familiar details of local interest. Those of us who have spent the most impressionable years of our life working, camping, and wandering among the fells and dales know well the incomparable freedom and beauty of the wild and less accessible parts of the district. At the same time, any valuation of the Lakeland Landscape would be unbalanced were we to ignore the less dramatic, but no less beautiful countryside on its fringe, for it welcomes the visitor as he approaches the mountains from any direction.

Whereas Nature still remains untamed in many parts of the region, and exposes the physical structure of her primæval form, elsewhere the scenery has been shaped and modified by the work of generations of men, and the result is there expressed in a softer pastoral landscape where stone or whitewashed villages and farms harmonize perfectly and provide human scale and interest.

If, so far, the cherished lakes and fells which we describe have escaped for the most part the ruthless industrial activity and disfigurements of the nineteenth century, our gratitude is due in no small measure to that stalwart band of writers and poets who opened the eyes of the nation to the inherited beauty of their land. The "Friends of the Lake District" are indeed only translating into action the call of men like Wordsworth, Ruskin, Rawnsley, and many others whose remains now lie under the shadow of ancient churches in Lakeland valleys.

CONTENTS

ILLUSTRATIONS

MAPS AND DIAGRAMS

A NOTE ON THE MAPS AND DIAGRAMS

THE KEY MAP at the beginning of the book shows the relation of the Lake District to neighbouring counties, and the main road communications. The CONTOUR DIAGRAM (facing page 6) serves to indicate the most prominent physical features. The GEOLOGICAL DIAGRAM (facing page 20) shows to a small scale the main geological divisions of the District ; it should be read in conjunction with the Contour Diagram and the coloured Landscape Map, which is folded at the end of the book.

The LANDSCAPE MAP represents the result of a comparative analysis of English scenery in different counties and its application to the Lake District. The method adopted for its presentation in distinctive colours follows the system used by the authors in the other books of this series already published. The map has been simplified to present a clear picture of the general landscape character of the District to a scale appropriate to the size of the book. It has been found necessary, therefore, for the sake of clarity, to eliminate all the less important roads, and to include only the names of towns and larger villages, as well as the more important landscape features. For greater detail the reader, and especially those on walking tours, should refer to the one-inch scale maps published by the Ordnance Survey Office or by Bartholomew.

The authors recognize that it is impossible and undesirable to formulate a rigid scale of values in terms of landscape beauty, as the emotional response of man to scenery is personal and variable. Nevertheless, certain kinds of scenery, whether wild or cultivated, have a greater human appeal than others, and they may differ considerably in character. For this reason the various landscape features have been indicated on the map as follows :

1. *Country of special landscape value :*
   (*a*) Rural areas below 1250 feet coloured yellow.
   (*b*) Fells and moorlands 1250 to 2500 feet coloured light brown.
   (*c*) High fells above 2500 feet coloured dark brown.
2. *Important woodlands coloured green.*
3. *National Trust properties.* The larger ones are hatched with a green line and the small properties shown by a green triangle.
4. *Towns and villages* are shown by black squares or diagonal black line hatching.
5. *Characteristic towns and villages* which are, in general, unspoilt by incongruous building are coloured red.
6. *Towns and villages of special interest* are also enclosed by a red ring.
7. *Churches and abbeys* of particular interest are indicated by a red cross.
8. *Ancient monuments* are marked by a small red ring.

The minor roads and principal fell tracks are indicated by a single broken line to differentiate them from the main motor roads which are shown by a double line. Lakes and tarns are coloured blue.

I

THE LAKELAND LANDSCAPE

I. CHARACTERISTICS OF THE LAKE DISTRICT

FEW men have understood the beauty of the Lakeland landscape more clearly than Wordsworth, who spent so many days of his life walking along the melodious river valleys or wandering happily over the rough mountain tracks. His *Guide through the Lake District* is inspired by a deep insight into the spiritual and historic background which, together with the superb hill scenery, has made this one of the happiest and most hospitable regions in the British Isles. He lived in an age exempt from modern noise and turmoil, when the Lake District, though beginning to be a resort for tourists, was a comparatively remote region. It is interesting, therefore, to find that descriptions written so long ago as 1835 fit, without material alteration, so much of the Lakeland scenery.

Immediately the traveller leaves the main road at Levens Bridge or Kendal and turns westward he becomes aware of a gentleness in the scene and a friendliness in the air. The Pennine Chain no longer dominates the landscape, and instead the traveller rides between the sloping sides of the fells. Becks rush noisily over stony beds ; picturesque groups of trees rise out of rocky outcrops in the fertile meadows ;

cattle feed in the valleys and sheep graze the rougher hillsides, and between these two feeding grounds on well-chosen sites, shielded by solid clumps of sycamore, lie stone and lime-washed farmhouses with silver-green slate roofs. It is a landscape of perfect harmony, increasing in variety of contour and richness of colour as the traveller approaches the central mountain groups.

The Lake District is formed on a wheel-like pattern, with a central hub of high fells composed of hard volcanic rock, long ridges for spokes, and lakes and dales occupying the spaces. A study of the map at the end of this book will clearly demonstrate this, and it is a formation which will soon become familiar to the visitor. At the heads of the western dales, he will find his passage blocked by the mountains grouped round Scafell, but by the Honister Pass, by Whinlatter or Buttermere Hause, he can gain access to Derwentwater and the central road which bisects the Lake District from north to south. On the eastern fringe of the district, again, he will find the ends of the valleys closed by high mountains.

Generally speaking, the English Lake District is a well-defined area of some 700 square miles, bounded on the west by Solway Firth and the Irish Sea, and on the north by the rolling green plain which stretches out towards Carlisle and the wild moorlands of the Border; it is only on the east that it is joined to the massive central plateau of the Pennine Chain by those bleak uplands known as Shap Fells, Langdale Fell, and Ravenstonedale Common.

A glance at the map will show that the higher fells

are arranged fan-wise above Coniston and Windermere, with an isolated mass to the north around Skiddaw and Saddleback. They may be divided roughly into five main groups. On the extreme east lies the High Street Range, less known perhaps than the others, and containing some of the loneliest dales and the remotest fell scenery of the region. Next to it, travelling westward, stands Helvellyn, bold and craggy, with Fairfield to protect it on the south and Great Dodd on the north. Beyond it lie Saddleback and Skiddaw. To the west again lie the Brackenthwaite Fells and the Derwent Fells in all the glory of their broken silhouettes: and lastly, to the south-west, peak behind peak rise the wildest and noblest hills of them all—Scafell and Scafell Pike, Great Gable, Bowfell, The Pillar, with many others whose names are familiar to climbers. They are wild and forbidding, cold, grey, and ominous in stormy weather, or irresistibly inviting in the glory of a summer's day. Attached to them but forming what might be termed a sub-group are the Coniston Fells, The Old Man, Wetherlam, Swirl How, and Grey Friar.

Each of these groups has a distinctive character. Skiddaw and Saddleback are magnificent rivals, the one elegantly concave and the other ruggedly convex. The former is superb in sunny weather when blue cloud shadows sweep across its grassy slopes. Saddleback, on the other hand, impresses in wilder weather when the clouds are low and the craggy summit is a deep indigo behind the yellow-brown shoulders. It is seen clearly at close range from the village of Threlkeld and the Keswick-Penrith road.

Whereas the Skiddaw group is formed as a definite circle of hills, the Helvellyn range is long and ridge-like, with its massive western slope cut into by more than a dozen steep gills, which fall like silver ribbons down the hill sides. On its eastern side, glaciers and the weather have formed a series of long and lovely dales leading down to Ullswater ; Grizedale, Glenridding, Glencoyne, and Deep Dale are a quartette of curving valleys which afford everchanging views both of Helvellyn itself and of its supporting hills.

East of the Helvellyn range and separated from it by the Kirkstone Pass lies the High Street group. High Street itself takes its name from the Roman road which traverses the level summit and drops down to Troutbeck and Windermere. It is a long hill ending dramatically above Hayeswater, which lies in one of the most lonely valleys where the wild red deer feeds on the rough grass. Ill Bell, Thornthwaite Crag, and Caudale Moor are unsurpassed in beauty of outline by any other Lakeland fells. They stand surrounding the head of the Troutbeck valley, a wide, grassy amphitheatre, and their silhouettes softly curved with long undulating ridgelines. The valley of the river Kent and Long Sleddale repeat in their own way the sweeping lines and swelling curves which characterize the hills of this region. Mardale, at the head of Haweswater, is surrounded by wilder amd more rugged scenery, and in spite of the activities of the Manchester Corporation, is bound to retain much of its grandeur, especially when the sky is wild and the clouds are low.

We come now to our last two mountain groups, the

Brackenthwaite and Derwent Fells, and Scafell and its wild and magnificent neighbours.

The Brackenthwaite Fells and the Derwent Fells lie on the western edge of the Lake District. Seen in the soft light of a summer evening across Derwentwater, they form a fairyland of peaks and ridges. They appear to increase in height; their slopes become a soft grey blue, oddly transparent; the sky above them glows a silvered yellow, and the gentle mist rising from the water and mingling with the shadowland of woods and valleys transfigures the whole.

The immense crags of Honister form a grand outpost to the last and highest group. Here we can forget the small scale of our English mountains and the soft gentle aspect of the greater part of Lakeland scenery. Instead we find ourselves in a world of rocky peaks and deep stony valleys: of flying clouds and sudden storms of rain or sleet: in a world, indeed, where we may be forced to fight with determination against a gale of wind or a thick mist. Scafell Pike, the highest mountain in England, forms the nodal point of this impressive star-like formation of high fells. On many days the summit is hidden by cloud. On all days it is characterized by a dignified aloofness as it stands surrounded by a protecting circle of the giants among the Lakeland hills, and there is an air of defiance about Scafell and its peers, dominating their stony valleys, indifferent to man and his puny works.

Seven valleys lead into the heart of the Scafell group: Borrowdale, the Buttermere Valley, Ennerdale, Wasdale, Eskdale, Dunnerdale, and Langdale.

All begin among soft gentle hills with vivid green meadows and pleasant homely farmhouse groups and end in treeless volcanic mountains, where the wind and Atlantic rainstorms sweep across the summits with a vindictive power of penetration. In sunny weather the hills stand out warm coloured and clear cut, but it is astonishing how quickly the storm-clouds can race in from the south-west and obliterate all but the lower slopes.

Gripped in their mountain settings, like jewels of turquoise or emerald, lie the lakes and dales. No other tract of country can show so much variety of scenery in so small an area. Contrast, for example, Windermere with its soft, low contoured hills and densely wooded shores, with Wastwater, grim, silent, and dark, with scarcely a tree to relieve the sombre dignity of its surroundings. Or again, consider the remote inaccessible beauty of Ennerdale, with its long narrowing valley of the river Liza penetrating far into the hills under Great Gable, and compare it to the busy scene on the banks of Grasmere, itself a lake of cultivated beauty. Think again of Ullswater beginning in the north-east with a park-like landscape of level meadows and large trees and ending near Patterdale among steep, precipitous hills and thickly wooded crags.

In all there are a score of lakes, not counting the numerous little tarns on the fells. Two of them have become reservoirs for the Corporation of Manchester and lost something of the primitive charm which belongs to a landscape carved by Nature alone and adorned by the sympathetic handiwork of man with

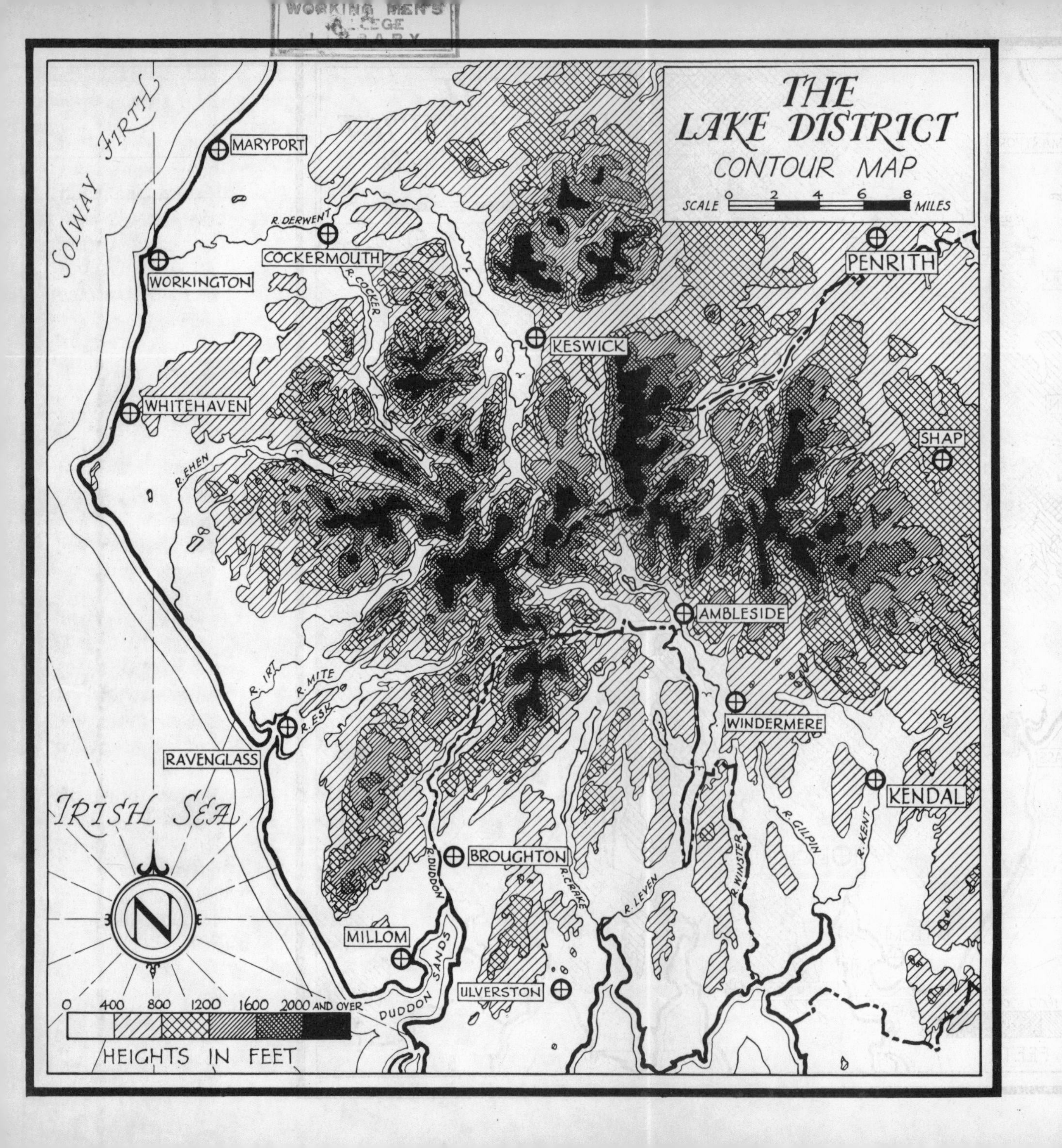
THE LAKE DISTRICT
CONTOUR MAP
SCALE 0 2 4 6 8 MILES
SOLWAY FIRTH
MARYPORT
R. DERWENT
COCKERMOUTH
WORKINGTON
R. COCKER
KESWICK
PENRITH
WHITEHAVEN
SHAP
R. EHEN
AMBLESIDE
R. IRT
R. MITE
R. ESK
WINDERMERE
RAVENGLASS
KENDAL
IRISH SEA
R. GILPIN
R. KENT
R. DUDDON
BROUGHTON
R. CRAKE
R. LEVEN
R. WINSTER
N
MILLOM
DUDDON SANDS
ULVERSTON
0 400 800 1200 1600 2000 AND OVER
HEIGHTS IN FEET

bridges, boundary walls, and dwellings. It seems a little odd that the storms which soak the lofty summits of Helvellyn and High Street and beat down upon the hapless tourist unlucky enough to be caught without protection, should pour serenely forth from some suburban tap in Manchester! But if this unhappy thought should upset us while passing Thirlmere, where flocks of Herdwick sheep have given place to the Corporation plantations, let us pass on to Derwentwater and enjoy the delicate beauty of its serene stretch of water, lying peacefully beneath the craggy and well-wooded slopes of High Seat and the long vigorous ridge of Cat Bells. Of all the English lakes Derwentwater is the most popularly beautiful. Unlike the other lakes it has breadth as well as length; unlike the others it is surrounded by hills and has no anti-climax in its setting.

It would be difficult to arrange the lakes in any order of merit as regards their beauty, for each has an individual character. Ennerdale, for example, seen from its western end, appears to lie in the heart of its mountainous surroundings: it can boast none of those rocky promontories and islands clothed with trees which adorn Windermere and Derwentwater. Instead it has a purity of line in its landscape which excels every other lake, and there are few more moving scenes in the whole Lake District than the vision of Ennerdale from the garden of the Angler's Inn. Bassenthwaite Lake is tame by comparison, and is only saved from dullness by the proximity of Skiddaw and the Lorton Fells. Of the other lakes, Crummock and Buttermere lie deeply seated among the fells, linked by a flat patch of green meadowland characteristic of the valleys. They have an air of silent remoteness in spite of the increased traffic on Honister Pass, which so dramatically brings the tourist, after a wild descent past rocks and screes, to the level shore. Coniston Water relies on the noble outline of the Coniston Fells and a thickly wooded eastern shore for its effect. Esthwaite and Elterwater are both quiet stretches of water with reedy banks, the haunt of wild fowl : Grasmere and Rydal Water, better known possibly than all the others save Windermere, combine the lyrical beauty of Derwentwater with the peacefulness of Esthwaite.

This outline of the characteristics of the Lake District would be incomplete without some reference to its increasing use and popularity for summer holidays. This not only has created difficulties in dealing with the seasonal influx of traffic, but it has had a marked effect on building developments and the local industry of catering for tourists of all classes, who visit the district by motor coach and car, or on bicycle and walking tours.

In the holiday months motor cars invade the narrow valleys in greater numbers than make for peace, as they do in all the more beautiful corners of England where access by road, however narrow, exists. This fact has created a strong antipathy to the motoring tourist in the minds of old lovers of the Lake District, who object for good reasons to the " opening up " of by-ways and mountain tracks in the central areas ; moreover, thousands who spend their brief holidays on the fells and lakes wish to escape from the over-mechanized conditions of the great cities. Yet, for reasons of advancing age or otherwise, there are many who wish to visit old haunts by car, and who no longer have the strength or leisure to climb and walk ; therefore if, as we hope, the Lake District is to become the first of our National Parks, it must be accessible to all who wish to enjoy the beauty it can offer, whether by car, bicycle, or on foot, provided that the central high fells are not disturbed by through traffic.

The keen walker will in this way retain the complete freedom of the unenclosed mountains and the bracken-covered fells. His alone will be the privilege to roam at will like the little Herdwicks on their high pastures, or follow up the age-old tracks from the valley farms to the more bracing air on the fell-tops. By so doing he can pass easily from one dale-head to another, and can enjoy the thrills and satisfaction unknown to those who must follow the valley roads by car or motor coach.

On the other hand, there is some compensation for the motorist who wishes to make a rapid tour of the district, as he can experience an immense variety of scenery in a short time and on the same day. He is able to leave Bowness just as the morning mists lift from the warming surface of Windermere and the blue smoke of chimneys rises vertically above the grey roofs. Crossing the ferry he can pass through the woodlands of Sawrey and by the serene margins of Esthwaite Lake to Hawkshead, still asleep in the morning haze ; and as he climbs over the hill beyond the little town there will be revealed the glorious panorama at the head of Windermere, the immense horseshoe of Fairfield, and the grand silhouette of the

High Street range above Kirkstone. As he descends to the head of Coniston Lake he can watch the shadows moving across the craggy slopes of the " Old Man," before turning to follow the highly coloured valley road under Yewdale Fells to Skelwith Bridge and over Red Bank to Grasmere by an abrupt descent to the lake side. From Grasmere he can climb smoothly over Dunmail Raise and see the bold mass of Helvellyn rising proudly over Thirlmere, and then pass on through the emerald meadows of St. John's Vale which lies so snugly under the brown slopes of Great Dodd. As he emerges from the northern end of this entrancing valley there will appear the noble outline of Saddleback against the northern sky, and then, turning towards Keswick, he can peep into the dark little valley of the Glenderaterra Beck and see beyond the long shoulders of Skiddaw. After a midday halt at Portinscale or Keswick, the tourist can take the lovely road round the western shore of Derwentwater with a grand prospect of the "jaws of Borrowdale" and the superb background of Glaramara. Crossing the Derwent at Grange Bridge the Borrowdale road will lead him past those exquisite birches on the riverside where a narrow defile serves as a prelude to the wide level meadows of Rosthwaite and Seatoller. Honister Pass is now open to the motorist, although there are easier alternative routes from Keswick over Buttermere Hause or Whinlatter to the Buttermere Valley and Crummock. From Crummock he can skirt the unfrequented shores of Loweswater, and so round the foot of the fells by Lamplugh village to Ennerdale. Surely here it is best to spend the night in order to have the unforgettable experience of watching the sun rise and throw its silvery shafts of light across the lake, and slowly awaken the sleeping fells.

On the western fringe of the Lake District, the motorist will find himself between mountains and sea. He can take an attractive fell road to Calder Abbey, opening up views to the Solway Firth across a foreground of sloping green fields or brown moorland. From Calder Bridge he can make for Gosforth and then turn into Wasdale and penetrate far into the heart of the mountains, but he will be compelled to return along the same road, if he wishes to approach Eskdale by Sauton Bridge and Eskdale Green. Finally, he can drive round the great landmark of Black Combe and, crossing the head of the Duddon estuary, complete his circuit by Coniston and Ambleside to Windermere. Thus the motorist may gain a general impression of the central and western lakes, while his walking rival will have acquired a more intimate knowledge and more lasting memories of some particular valley and its surrounding heights.

For many the best way of seeing the Lake District is to combine the convenience of a motor with the never-ending joy of walking. The whole region is organized to this end. Everywhere can be found comfortable hotels or simple farmhouse lodgings, where the hospitable folk of these northern counties will entertain the visitor in their inimitable way. In fact, the local hotels and inns are a distinct feature of the Lakeland landscape, and many are old posting houses and coaching inns. Built of stone like the "Old

England" at Bowness, or colour-washed a bright yellow or clean white like the "Derwentwater" at Portinscale or the "Swan" at Grasmere, they stand out at intervals below the green sloping hillsides or reflected in the surface of a lake. No other district of its size is so well equipped with inns, many of them excellent. They range from large country houses like Armathwaite Hall, Bassenthwaite, and Storrs Hall, Windermere, to tiny inns like the Kirkstone Pass Inn, set so high among the hills, or the Barngate Inn, famous for its view over the hills round Windermere, or the "Woolpack" in Eskdale with its tree-shaded forecourt.

The most typical Lakeland hotels were built some decades ago in the local materials, or are sympathetic enlargements of older and smaller buildings. Such are the Derwentwater Hotel at Portinscale with its perfect garden leading down towards the reedy banks of the lake, and Low Wood on the eastern shore of Windermere. From the sloping garden of Low Wood, with its fine shrubs and trim lawns, there is a magnificent view across the lake to Wetherlam and the Langdale Pikes. The Crown Hotel at Bowness has an enviable site above the main street of the village, looking out over the whole panoramic lay-out of the lake and mountains. Other notable hotels are the Ullswater and Patterdale, which again possess interesting gardens; the latter, indeed, has one of the finest natural rock gardens, where intense blue patches of gentian mingle in the autumn with the browns, reds, and greens of maple, berberis, and other familiar shrubs. The "Prince of Wales" on Grasmere and the Keswick

Hotel both deserve great praise ; moreover the latter is notable for a very remarkable collection of coloured cartoons. Although it is not our intention to anticipate the reader's own discoveries, we cannot leave the subject without mentioning the Mortal Man Inn at Troutbeck, with its discriminating landlord ; the comforts of the old Wild Boar Inn near Crook : the Swan Hotel at Newby Bridge standing by its exquisite river scene : the Howtown Hotel on the eastern shore of Ullswater, splendid headquarters for exploring the High Street group of hills : the Skelwith Bridge Hotel facing another river scene, and the charming inn at Scalehill, near Crummock. Mention has already been made of the Angler's Hotel on the very edge of Ennerdale Lake, most beautifully sited of them all and enjoying the solitude of the high fells ; and there are the hospitable hotels in Borrowdale and Langdale, useful to the walker and climber. Of the remainder there are many unnamed here which will come immediately to the mind of the reader, equally good and comfortable, and of unpretentious design.

Gardens, whether belonging to hotels or private houses, are a distinctive feature of the landscape. The warm moist western atmosphere is favourable to such richly coloured shrubs as the Japanese maple, which can be seen to perfection on many hillsides. Azaleas and rhododendrons also flourish and form vivid pictures in the early summer. May and June indeed are the best months for colour as the trees are clothed in the first fresh green, while in succession are spread the carpets of wild daffodils and bluebells and clumps of crimson foxgloves. In the autumn too, in a favourable year, the rich tints in such favoured spots as Coniston's Yewdale, Derwentwater, and Gowbarrow Park, Ullswater, are beyond description. Maple, birch, bracken, alder, holly, and yew combine with the craggy hill backgrounds or the blue lake water to form incredible symphonies of colour. Later still, when the highest hills are white with snow, the lower fells a brilliant copper with dead bracken, and the meadows still a vivid green, there is no more beautiful sight in any part of the British Isles.

Atmospheric effects enhance the beauty of the Lakeland landscape to a far greater extent than in less mountainous country. The evening light on the Derwent Fells has already been described with its softening effect on the silhouette of the hills. On one of those supreme days after rain this is entirely reversed and all the hills stand out clear cut with every crag and ravine plainly visible, and from the highest fells the panorama extends far and wide to the Yorkshire Pennines, the Isle of Man, and Scotland. In strange contrast are the more frequent soft, wet days when only the lower slopes of the hills are visible and the summits are draped in a thick cotton-wool mantle of cloud. At such times the road round Loughrigg along the banks of the Rotha holds a mysterious charm, for the river fills the visible world with the music of its rushing water, the trees are bejewelled with crystal drops on all their branches, and our attention is focused on the more intimate world beneath the clouds ; we can enjoy the wagtail on its stone or the flight of the swallow as it skims the boulders in the river bed. And the Lake District is full of details—a group of lambs standing proudly on some miniature crag : a shepherd and his dog collecting his flock in a sloping field : a little stone bridge leaping its stream in one graceful arch : long walls alive with a variety of ferns : sleeping villages and isolated farms : gabled boathouses half-hidden among the rushes of a lake-shore : tiny churches and snug white-washed inns : in short, a thousand and one harmonious touches which combine to create the Lakeland scene.

Around this complex region of mountains, fells, and lakes there is a fringe of sea, estuary, and moorland. Few lovers of the Lake District realize that the sea plays an important part in the composition of its western landscape. Here a sandy beach extends, backed by low dunes from which there are sweeping views to Black Combe in the south, and eastwards across the rolling foreground of fields to where the mountains rise in serried ranks, their summits more often than not hidden in the clouds. On the southern fringe again the long sandy estuaries of Morecambe Bay and the Duddon, with their abundance of bird-life, introduce an entirely different feature. Here these penetrating fingers of the sea, with their muddy tidal channels and their marshy shores, contrast strikingly in their pale greens or soft yellows with the richer reds and browns of the fell-sides or the inky sableness of Black Combe. On the north the fringe consists of a rolling plain of green meadows stretching out towards Solway Firth and Carlisle, and hides within its folds little stone villages with coloured windows and doorways and slate roofs. Caldbeck, for example, where the river everlastingly fills the church with the sound of running water, is a typical northern village. From there can be explored the northern slopes of the Skiddaw group of fells, and the high moorland so reminiscent of the Lammermuirs in Scotland. Penrith, twelve miles south-east of Caldbeck, commands the entrance to Ullswater as well as the great north road to Carlisle, and is an excellent centre from which to visit the eastern lakes or the wild tract of country near Shap, where the road rises steadily between coloured posts and where in winter the snow lies deep. Here the Lake District melts imperceptibly into the Pennine landscape in a series of hills growing bleaker and less friendly to the traveller; a treeless expanse of moorland country, strangely beautiful or cruel according to the weather or the time of year.

So far we have not attempted more than to sketch the characteristics of so intricate a region—a land of high open fells and rivers ; lowland country stretching out to the sea ; lakes deep set in the mountains or richly set in wooded meadowland ; tracks for the walker, winding roads for the motorist, with everywhere the welcoming inn and the hospitable farmhouse. In summer it is a world of happy pilgrims, rich or poor, who come to the hills to regain something of that eternal strength which the crowded city does more each year to sap. But underneath this scenic world of moving clouds and challenging mountains lies a stern world of fact, where the farmer earns a bare livelihood in the valleys, and the shepherd staggers forth in winter on to the fell sides to find his missing ewes under deep drifts of snow. A world which has reared the hardy and self-disciplined dalesman with a soft speech and keen eye, who regards the visitor as a crop in the rotation, appearing in late spring with the green shoots and disappearing in autumn when the bracken is being cut. To him the mountains are sheep-runs and sometimes obstacles ; the towns, markets ; and the villages or farmhouses, home. It is impossible both to be part of and to look at a landscape. The shepherds and the farmer are of it, the visitor outside it, and it is solely because the Lakeland landscape is so impregnable in its grandeur that it can absorb so many alien invasions during the more crowded months of summer.

2. THE GEOLOGICAL FOUNDATION

When we are travelling about the country by train or motor, gliding swiftly and smoothly on a man-made track of steel or asphalt, it is difficult to relate our fleeting impressions of a visual world to the unseen matter beneath us. It is not easy to dissociate ourselves from our mechanized environment and realize the stuff of which worlds are made. The farmer and all workers on the soil are more aware of such matters, for they have gained, by hard-won struggles against Nature, a practical knowledge of surface soils and water-bearing subsoils, and the kind of crops and vegetation these will support. For many, an interest in geology is only stimulated by an occasional experience in contact with some exceptional natural feature where the structure of earth is revealed. Who has not been thrilled on approaching England by a sight of the "Seven Sisters," their white forms rising above the Channel and leading the eye homewards along the gentle contours of smooth chalk downs? There are many other examples of places where we feel compelled to take an interest in geology—as, for instance, at the great quarries of Portand, where heroic blocks of glistening stone lie hewn from their natural bed before they are transported to ennoble the architecture of our cities. Then there are those immense China Clay pits and pyramids in Cornwall where the white decomposed granite is exposed to view, so different from the titanic blocks of hard granite which form the cliffs at Land's End and magnificently defy the Atlantic. In the lovely gorge at Cheddar and the mysterious caves of Wookey we can examine the structure of Magnesium Limestone fully exposed on the escarpment of the Mendips. So, too, as you pass north-eastward across England from the Cotswolds, the oölitic rocks are expressed in the characteristic scenery and echoed in the old stone villages. Travelling by rail to the north through Derbyshire or Yorkshire the intimate connection between the rock outcrops and the landscape is apparent in every cutting or quarry, in the fence walls and village buildings. There are subtle changes in colouring and vegetation as you pass through the variety of Carboniferous Limestone rocks of the Pennines, as here and there the Millstone Grit gives a more sombre appearance to the countryside. As the southern fringe of the Lake District is approached the light grey limestone crags are left behind, and we enter a region of much older rocks, and the district of low fells which lead us towards the grand mountain massifs of Cumbria. Even a superficial knowledge of geology gives added interest to walking in this lovely district, for in whatever part of it you may choose to wander, on the lower fells or high mountains, the nature of the rocks emphasize the variations in landscape beauty.

No man surely could fail to be impressed by the contemplation of the great drama of creation which, through long acts of stupendous earth-movements and intervals of quiescence, lasted more than 400 million years until, in the final scene, was produced the panorama of mountain and lake, of fell and dale much as we see it to-day. Only at the very end of the great drama appeared man on the stage to humanize the scene with his dwellings and flocks and cultivation.

Let us go back to the first act of the drama, to what is known as the Ordovician Period which, in its various phases, lasted perhaps 60 million years and during which all the "old rocks," forming the greater part of the Lake District, began to take shape. Firstly, we may imagine the "Skiddaw Slates," perhaps several thousand feet in thickness, being slowly deposited in a shallow sea in the form of muddy and sandy sediments over the whole region. This tranquil phase was followed by the second—one of intense volcanic activity—when lavas, in the form mostly of andesites, were poured out, and older fragments of solid rock combined with fluid lavas to form agglomerates like coarse concrete. These rocks constitute what are now known as the "Borrowdale Series" by reason of the fact that somewhere in the heart of the Lake District, and probably Borrowdale, was the centre of volcanic action. During the third phase both the Skiddaw Slates and the Borrowdale volcanic rocks were subject, over a long period, to a powerful process of uplift and folding, and continuous erosion of the surface, before the later rock formations were deposited, namely, the Coniston Limestone and the Silurian Rocks which now appear in the landscape of the southern portion of the District (*see* Geological Diagram).

Some of the volcanic rocks were subject to terrific compression and folding, so producing the splendid beds of rocks which are now mined and split for roofing slates at the Honister Crag workings. It was sometime in this period also that the buried masses of igneous rock were forced up and appeared as intrusions on the surface, and so you may find in Eskdale the pinkish granite outcrops, and the granophyre of similar colour in the lower part of Ennerdale. Other intrusive granite outcrops occur near Skiddaw and at Shap.

The Lake District, as indeed the whole of Britain, subsequently passed through the long protracted period of movement and partial submergence when the later formations of rocks were deposited on the fringe of the fell country. In what is known to geologists as the Tertiary period, earth-movements and the "faulting" of rocks gave us the main outline of the district as we know it to-day. The "great dome" or central massif of Cumbria was forced up, forming the high fells around Scafell, Great Gable, and the adjoining summits, although these were denuded of their surface rocks, and so came into being the radiating valleys

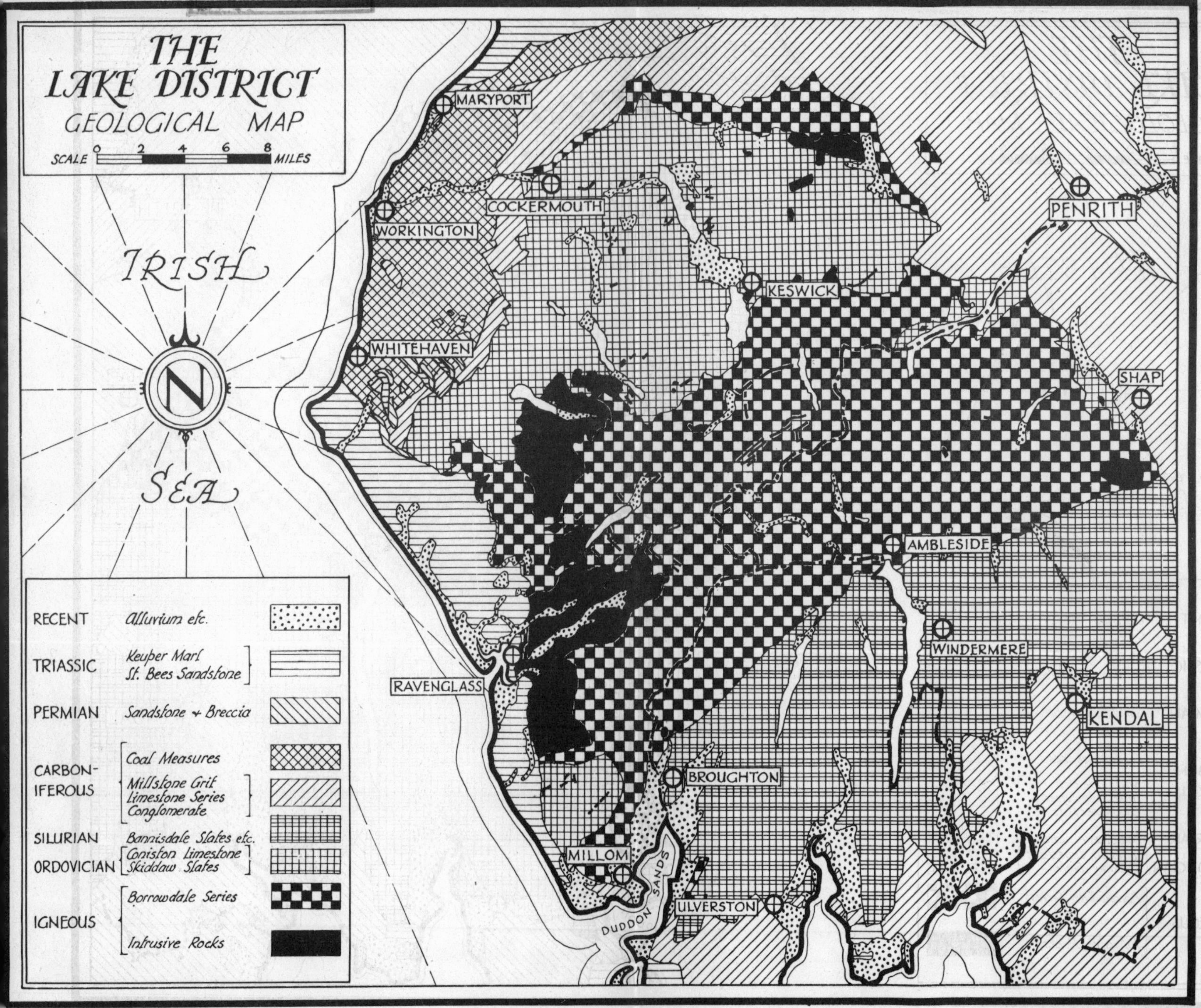
THE LAKE DISTRICT
GEOLOGICAL MAP
SCALE 0 2 4 6 8 MILES
IRISH
SEA
N
MARYPORT
COCKERMOUTH
WORKINGTON
WHITEHAVEN
KESWICK
PENRITH
SHAP
AMBLESIDE
WINDERMERE
KENDAL
RAVENGLASS
BROUGHTON
MILLOM
DUDDON SANDS
ULVERSTON
RECENT
Alluvium etc.
TRIASSIC
Keuper Marl
St. Bees Sandstone
PERMIAN
Sandstone + Breccia
CARBON-IFEROUS
Coal Measures
Millstone Grit
Limestone Series
Conglomerate
SILURIAN
Bannisdale Slates etc.
ORDOVICIAN
Coniston Limestone
Skiddaw Slates
IGNEOUS
Borrowdale Series
Intrusive Rocks

and watercourses which have their source in the highest of the volcanic mountains.

We may pass on to the Ice Age which followed. Evidence of this may still be seen in all the high dale-heads in the form of moraines—the debris of glaciers—as at Langstrath, Greenup, and Ennerdale, or in the deep glacial lakes of Wastwater and Ennerdale. As the melting ice scoured out the mountain-sides, carrying with it the surface rocks, it frequently dammed the valleys and becks and so imprisoned the high mountain tarns which are such a feature of this District. It must be remembered that this region was still covered by its mantle of ice and snow long after southern Britain was enjoying the milder conditions suitable for the maintenance of primæval life; hence it is not likely that the Lake District could provide a home for its first primitive settlements until the last of the glaciers had run its course and the dales had slowly acquired their green pasture and vegetation on the alluvial soil. Only then, in the last act of the drama of creation, appeared man to humanize the Lakeland scene, first as hunter and pioneer and later as herdsman and cultivator of the soil.

3. THE HUMAN CONTRIBUTION

For reasons already stated, the late period in which human settlements appeared in the District accounts for the comparatively few remains of early man. Yet the Neolithic and Bronze Age accounts for some notable monuments, and these have a superb setting unspoilt by the additions of a later time. Three stone circles may be mentioned. On Castle Rigg, near Keswick, is a fine example of fifty large stones, having as a background the noble mountains of Blencathra, Skiddaw, Helvellyn, and other high fells. "Long Meg and her Daughters" is another example near Penrith, while a third, also of large stones, will be found high up on the Swinside Fells above the Duddon estuary. Most authorities are of the opinion that these great stone circles were the places for meetings and assemblies connected with religious rites, which suggests some early form of social and religious organization dating back to the Bronze Age or possibly Neolithic times.

In addition to these notable examples, there is a smaller circle near Burnmoor on Eskdale Fell, also set in a scene of wild beauty, and a great many other remains of circles and cairns on the western fells. Hence even in pre-Roman times it may be assumed that considerable parts of the Lake District were colonized by primitive folk in tribal communities.

The power of ancient Rome left its impress even in such hazardous and difficult country, nor is this surprising when we realize the magnitude of the task in the construction of the great wall of Hadrian from Carlisle to Newcastle, and the need for communication with the Solway coast. Possibly during the passage of the expeditionary legions through the Lake District the native inhabitants would make use of strong positions and places of refuge known to them. In any case early British forts are believed to have existed in several places, for example, in Mardale: between Derwentwater and Thirlmere at the northern end of Bleaberry Fell; at Brownrigg near Great Mell

PREHISTORIC STONE CIRCLE, CASTLERIGG, KESWICK

Fell, and on Castle Crag commanding "the jaws of Borrowdale." These early British strongholds left little impression on the landscape, nor were they near the main lines of Roman communications. We have, however, closer evidence of Roman occupation, for their fortified camp sites remain near Penrith (BROVACUM), at Borrans near Ambleside (GALAVA), and at Hardknott which commands Eskdale and the route to the Roman harbour at Ravenglass (CLANOVENTA). Hardknott Castle, by reason of its superb site, is perhaps the most impressive of the examples mentioned.

During the dark ages the historian is silent on man's contribution to life in this region even although we know that St. Kentigern arrived in the district on his missionary travels. In mediæval times the power of the Church made its influence felt on the dales of Cumberland and Westmorland. There is the fine ruined abbey in its lovely setting by the Calder, and the abbey ruins at Shap, while the monks of Furness who owned property in Borrowdale and the neighbourhood of Esthwaite and Windermere established their granges and storehouses. Greystoke possesses a fine parish church, but more characteristic of Lakeland churches is the original parish church of Keswick at Crosthwaite, or those at Grasmere and Bowness (Windermere). It is, however, the simple little stone or whitewashed churches in the dales, beside their ancient yews, which have added so much unsophisticated charm to the landscape. With the utmost economy in material, and small in scale, these little churches such as Rosthwaite, Wasdale Head, Wythburn, and Ulpha, yet give just the right human note and centre of attraction to the small communities which they serve.

We have commented on the architecture of the district in Chapter VI. It is only necessary to mention here how much the landscape has been enriched by the farmhouses and humble dwellings of the dales. The comparative poverty of the men who built them, living a hard life as fell shepherds and small farmers, determined the local style of building which is simple in construction and of materials taken from the nearest quarry. It is rare to find any attempt at conscious ornamentation, although here and there survive interesting features like spinning galleries where the womenfolk used to spin and weave the garments of wool from their own flocks of Herdwick sheep.

Quarrying and mining have, at least from Elizabethan times, provided a livelihood for some of the village communities, and these activities have made a considerable impression on the appearance of hill and dale. In the sixteenth century a colony of Germans was established near Keswick for the mining and smelting of copper ore, and a few of their descendants may have intermarried with local families. The presence of hæmatite accounts for the old mine workings near Boot in the Eskdale granite; and there are old lead, copper, and zinc mine workings in the Vale of Newlands and at Brandelhow and Cat Bells (Derwentwater). The village of Threlkeld, near Blencathra, came into being as a mining village, so too that at Greenside Glenridding; indeed, the waste washings of the Greenside mine have left their visible marks in the delta at the head of Ullswater.

Most of the old mine-workings in Borrowdale high on the fellside were made for the extraction of graphite, and so developed the pencil industry at Keswick; but this is now abandoned and nature has gradually absorbed the old workings in the landscape of the valley. In the Caldbeck district the workings for barytes has had its effect on the natural scene, and the presence of the same material at Force Crag in Coledale may affect this valley, but could hardly damage the views from the Whinlatter road more than the new plantations of the Forestry Commissioners with their rigid lines of young conifers.

There are quarries for slate, granite, and other stone in many parts of the Lake District, and particularly at Honister, Coniston, and Elterwater the old and existing slate workings are plainly visible from a distance; but it cannot be said that these legitimate and necessary activities do much to mar the beauty of the countryside, as the stone extracted, and even the quarry tips, are of the same colour as the surrounding rock outcrops.

It remains to mention the effects of the modern highway engineering on the Lakeland scenery. Until quite recent years the narrow roads which served the district were all designed for horse-vehicles, or for the passage of pack-horses, cattle, and sheep, and enclosed by the characteristic dry walling of local stone, or unenclosed on the fell land. So most of them remain, but the huge motor coaches carrying tourists through the region have demanded wider and straighter highways when these were possible. The Kendal-Windermere-and-Keswick road now stretches its broad ribbon to carry modern traffic and a host of summer visitors, but for the most part the old roads and narrow twisting lanes remain as in Wordsworth's day, and the pony tracks over the fells and the outruns to the high rough pastures are still the only evidence of the adaptation of Nature to human needs.

The present generation has done most to modify the scenery of Lakeland in the face of determined opposition, by the conspicuous intrusion of overhead electricity grid lines, or plantations of trees alien to a district which is so small in scale, so exquisite in its delicate beauty, that every human addition must be regarded with suspicion until justified. John Ruskin, followed by Rawnsley and others, successfully resisted a further penetration of the Lake District by the advancing network of railways, with the result that all the rail-heads are fortunately outside the most beautiful parts of the district. Yet these railways in their turn brought about the importation of building materials foreign to the locality, and so the visitor sees to-day the little blotches of bright red machine-made roofing tiles on villas by the shores of Windermere and elsewhere, in a land which produces the finest and most beautiful grey and green slates that are in perfect harmony with the natural colours of the landscape.

II

THE HEART OF THE LAKE DISTRICT

To the enthusiastic rock-climber, the " heart of Lakeland " usually means the mountains and high fells around the heads of Wasdale, Langdale, Ennerdale, and the Buttermere Valley, where the crags and gulleys are composed of the hardest volcanic rocks, and so afford reliable holds for hands and climbing boots. It is also in this central part of the district when the fell-sides are partly shrouded by passing clouds, that there is the most striking illusion of immense scale and grandeur reminiscent of alpine scenery. Sunlit peaks seem to soar skywards to an astonishing height above the sea of valley mist which, as it lifts, exposes the almost primæval character of the dale-heads.

Yet if we regard the " Heart of Lakeland " from a wider angle, it actually embraces a much greater tract of country than the more localized objectives of English rock-climbers. Viewed from the summit of Helvellyn, for example, five distinct mountain masses, separated by deep valleys, dominate the scene. On the eastern side, entirely in Westmorland, are the high fells of the High Street Range : in the centre, shared by Westmorland and Cumberland, is the Helvellyn and

Fairfield Group: away to the north dominating the Vale of Keswick stand Skiddaw and Saddleback: then to the north-west the Grasmoor-Hindscarth Group of slate hills: and lastly, the most dramatic series of volcanic mountains of Cumbria comprised in the Scafell region. Each group has its distinctive characteristics and silhouette arising from geological structure. In each the outstanding summits approach or exceed a height of 3000 feet.

These five groups may be conveniently described in the order in which we might approach them on foot from Penrith or Shap, where we ask the reader to leave behind him both car and railway, and go with us and his rucksack among these "fraternal hills." Only on foot will he fully realize the mystery and sombre beauty of the mountains and the fascinating solitude of the dale-heads where no motor can penetrate.

I. THE HIGH STREET RANGE

If we were to cross the Lake District as the Roman Legions did on their way from Penrith to the head of Windermere and so over Wrynose and Hardknott to Ravenglass on the coast, our route would start from the Roman camp site, "BROVACUM" by the river Eamont, near Penrith, and so lead us with a gradual rise along the spine of the fells which separate Ullswater from the Lowther valley. This route (High Street) after leaving the road, about two miles from Lowther Bridge, crosses the head of the Elder Beck and other tributaries of Ullswater, and as a fell track, climbs gradually over Loadpot Hill and Red Crag to the top of High Raise and Kidsty Pike (2560), then falls before its final ascent to the inconspicuous summit of High Street (2718).

The more interesting, though less historical, route to the summit is on foot from Shap, which is perhaps the best of all ways by which to enter the Lake District. This approach to the fells is a good introduction as it leads you along the pleasant Lowther Valley by footpath through the hamlet of Keld and past the mediæval ruins of Shap Abbey, whence you may choose to cut across country into Swindale and over the fell to Mardale. There will be found the steep and direct ascent to the top of High Street. Alternatively, the Lowther Valley may be followed to Bampton, and thence by a track across Bampton Common to the ridge north of High Raise and Kidsty Pike. The Swindale route will give the stranger the pleasure of seeing his first real Lakeland valley; it lessens the disappointment of seeing the beautiful Hawes Water in process of conversion into a reservoir for Manchester, and, when finally the top of High Street is conquered, there will come the wonderful revelation of the western landscape, with apparently range upon range of mountains before you. There are several easy ascending tracks from Mardale to the High Street fells, the choice of which will depend on whether you may intend later to follow the Roman road by Thornthwaite Crag down to Garburn Pass and Troutbeck, or, instead, descend from the high plateau direct to Patterdale as a starting-point for the walk over Helvellyn. Our own inclination would be to make direct to Kidsty Pike from Mardale and keep on the fell-tops as long as possible, unless the clouds are low, before seeking the shelter of the Troutbeck Valley.

From Kidsty it is well worth while to continue north-west to the top of Rest Dodd in order to get the views of two delectable valleys, Bannerdale and Rampsgill, which run down to Ullswater. Hereabouts is a lovely series of little dales to explore at leisure without the encumbrance of a rucksack if your temporary home is at Howtown. But if your night's rest is to be at Troutbeck or Waterhead you must turn south before the sun gets low and continue over the smooth top of High Street to Thornthwaite Crag, where the rough column of stone will give the clue to your position. We have then left behind us the distant landscape of the Yorkshire Pennines and the long expanse of lower fells and moorland about Shap, but in the opposite direction towards the west we can look across Caudale Moor to the greater heights of Fairfield, St. Sunday Crag, Dollywaggon, and Helvellyn. Looking south-east, as the sun sets, there lies in front of you a superb panorama, a great amphitheatre of dark blue mountains with Windermere stretching out as a broad ribbon to the south and continuing the line of the Troutbeck Valley. Coniston Old Man and the Seathwaite Fells stand out unchallenged south of the Wrynose Gap, and to the north of these the eyes is led to the more ragged silhouettes of Crinkle Crags and Bowfell, in fact, to all the highest peaks in the Scafell group. It is here, from this comparatively modest height of Thornthwaite Crag (about 2500 feet), that the stranger will get his " curtain raiser " to the romantic arena of hill and dale which is the " Heart of the Lake District."

Of the particular range of hills on which we stand, the prominent shapes, as seen from the lowland country, are not provided by High Street itself, but by Thornthwaite Crag, Froswick, and Ill Bell, although if you approach these hills from Sleddale (which runs south-east) it is Harter Fell which stand up prominently to separate the passes of Gate Scarth and Nan Bield. Whereas Gate Scarth is the col (1900) between Mardale and Sleddale, the direct passage from Mardale to Kentmere follows the track over Nan Bield (2050). The Roman route from Thornthwaite will take you directly down to Troutbeck, but by following the ridge over Froswick and Ill Bell you will have the more exciting views from the top of the crags which command upper Kentmere, and you will arrive on the top of Garburn Pass before finally descending by the pony track to Troutbeck.

The scenery of this region consists of long grass-covered hills rising above narrow valleys. Towards the north-east, by Lowther and Askham, cultivated fields can be seen through which grassy tracks lead up to the open moorland slopes. Long Sleddale and the Kent Valley (which once possessed a lake, now drained) are typical examples of eastern dales where the road winds along the river bank and ends in a grand semi-circle of hills. Everywhere the landscape is rounded in outline with a velvety green surface seen to perfection on the slopes of Ill Bell. This ridge rises like an enormous rampart above the heads of the Troutbeck and Kentmere Valleys and extends northwards to meet Thornthwaite Crag and Caudale Head and form that superb amphitheatre which can be seen so well from the top of Troutbeck Tongue.

The western approaches to the High Street group are on the whole more dramatic. Let the visitor approach Hayeswater from the delightful hamlet of Lower Hartsop and he will be rewarded with wild views up Pasture Beck between Raven Crag and Gray Crag to the rocky summit of Caudale Moor. Indeed, if he is fortunate, he may see the red deer feeding on the slopes of Rest Dodd or proceeding in single file towards Angle Tarn. Most mountain tarns are wild and lonely and Hayeswater is no exception. It lies high among the hills reflecting the blue of the sky till a sudden approaching cloud blots out the whole horseshoe of dark mountains which frown down upon its ruffled surface.

The great central ridge of High Street is a landmark to be recognized in all northern views enjoyed from vantage points round Lake Windermere. It rises, a dark mass, above the gentler sloping foreground of fells, and though on the whole less known and less generally explored than the other lakeland groups, embraces scenery of the highest order, especially for those who prefer open undulating ridge lines to rugged mountain peaks.

2. THE HELVELLYN AND FAIRFIELD GROUP

This group of mountains and high fells forms the watershed between Thirlmere and Ullswater and can

HIGH STILE AND RED PIKE, BUTTERMERE

here be clearly defined by the main motor roads which form the boundaries of the region. Within the large oval area encompassed by these roads lies some of the grandest and most characteristic bits of rock and fell country. The approach to the summit of Helvellyn itself from its eastern side, either along Striding Edge or Swirrel Edge, provides a fittingly dramatic climax to the ascent, for here, and indeed all along the eastern side of the Helvellyn range, the landscape has been sculptured by ice and snow for countless centuries, whereas the western and southern sides of the mountains, exposed to the sun and kinder winds of the Atlantic, reflect more gentle modelling in their smooth contours.

The most unimaginative way to climb Helvellyn, and unfortunately the one recently adopted by hundreds of " arm-chair " tourists, is to travel by motor coach and car from Windermere or Keswick to Wythburn church and from there make a mass attack on the invisible summit. We only mention this method by way of warning to the reader of what to avoid if he ever hopes to enjoy the lonely grandeur of the mountains. This fine range of hills should be approached in a more adventurous mood, and two days spent on the tops in the Helvellyn and Fairfield district is little enough time to explore the country under varying conditions of cloud and sunlight. We suggest, therefore, that an easy day's fell-walking could be devoted to the southern end of the Helvellyn range, starting from Troutbeck, Low-wood, Waterhead, or Ambleside, and ending your day near the head of Ullswater. These hills, which embrace Rydal Fell,

Fairfield, Hart Crag, and Scandale Fell form the lofty horseshoe-shaped frame to the Rydal Beck valley, and they provide the climax to all northward views from the upper half of Windermere. Between them and the lake is Wansfell, in the middle distance, leading the eye towards the summit and supporting hills of Fairfield.

If your day's walk over Fairfield to Ullswater begins at Troutbeck village, there is an easy path which leads you on to Wansfell Pike, and opens up the view westward to Little Langdale. Along this dale the Roman road passed from the head of Windermere to the coast, climbing over Wrynose and Hardknott Passes. On the left of this gap to the Cumberland dales stand up the fells above Coniston—Wetherlam, Old Man, and the rest.

After leaving Wansfell and crossing the Ambleside-Kirkstone road a long tongue of fell faces you separating Scandale from Kirkstone Pass. By following the high ground you may mount over Snarker Fell to the summit just above Red Screes and so command the long view of Patterdale and Brothers Water. Down below you throb the labouring engines of touring coaches and cars which appear from above like black beetles making their way over the 1500 feet of the Kirkstone climb. Looking eastward from this high vantage point above the pass one sees across the head of Troutbeck the familiar outline of the High Street range—Thornthwaite Crag (our excellent viewpoint yesterday), Froswick, and Ill Bell. Away to the south are the smooth waters of Windermere reflecting the summer sky. Imagine this scene as winter approaches. The brightly coloured bracken and vivid green patches of wet fell-side are transformed by a snowy mantle, covering all the high fells. Dark grey rocks and steep crags punctuate the wintry landscape, but the pattern of fence walls which mark the " intakes " from the fell are almost obliterated by deep snow-drifts. Yet winter does not always thus transform the Lakeland scene. We have memories of many an exciting day's fox-hunting over the country you will traverse to-day. The " Shepherd's Hunt " on Boxing Day, when the meet has so often been held at the Kirkstone Inn, provides a strange contrast for those whose hunting experience is in the shires. Here there may be only a small company of enthusiasts on foot—dalesmen, shepherds, and other local folk—who have already tramped some miles to the meet. Only the hounds, master, and weather-beaten huntsman give a touch of formality and colour to the scene. From your high position above the pass you would command a raven's view of the scene as hounds move off to the crags and screes where Reynard himself may be a spectator hiding among the rocks. It is strenuous work keeping up with a Lakeland Hunt in full cry after a strong mountain fox, and as likely as not he may lead young hounds to their death over the crags, or so fast that even the agile huntsman and young dalesmen never arrive for the kill on the slopes of Helvellyn. Some hounds may return to kennels alone after nightfall, while tired and perhaps rain-soaked followers eventually call in for a yarn and tankard of ale by the welcome fireside of some remote inn before dispersing to their distant homes. But to return to our walk over

Fairfield. The track, such as it is, from Red Screes strikes north-west across the top of Scandale Pass and then mounts quickly to the cairn above Dove Crags. It follows the high ground over Hart Crag and finally takes you to the top of Fairfield (2863). Southward, below you, is the green Rydal valley almost encircled by the opposing arms of Scandale Fell on the left hand and Rydal Fell on the right. Immediately below you to the west of Fairfield is Grisedale Tarn and beyond it the zig-zag track leading up to Dollywaggon Pike and Helvellyn. Our way lies due north till clear of the crags, then, bearing towards the high ground to the north-east, we reach the finely shaped summit of St. Sunday Crag. The whole of this walk is easy going and magnificent in its command of wide prospects in all directions, for there is but little dead ground to obstruct the views down all the valleys which run either to Grasmere or Patterdale. The only warning necessary is that when mist and clouds descend, beware of the crags on the Patterdale side of the range, for these occur in many places to the right of the ridge from Dove Crag to the summit of Fairfield. If it is found necessary to return for the night to Grasmere from the top of Fairfield follow the track due south, keeping on the high ground until it meets Greenhead Gill ; but if the weather has turned really foul on the summit it is better to descend to Grisedale Tarn and thence follow the good pony track either to the main road above Grasmere or to Patterdale. Our choice, given fair weather, is to continue north over the abrupt edge of Cofa Pike and then bear north-east to St. Sunday Crag where the views towards Ullswater will

HONISTER CRAG AND PASS

entice you to spend the night in Patterdale. The wooded hillsides of Glenridding on the west side of the lake and high fells to the east, which mask Boardale, frame an altogether delightful picture of the valley as you descend and finally emerge on the main road at the bottom of Grisedale. It will be an evening well spent by the lovely shores of Ullswater. If light remains after your evening meal and a day on the fells, row down the lake and look back to that wonderful frame of encircling hills which protect the head of the dale. To the south-west, Helvellyn has already received his night-cap of cloud, and on the dark slumbering form of St. Sunday Crag it is no longer possible to locate the route by which you descended. Over the placid waters of the lake itself falls the mist of a summer's night. Even the leisurely dip of your blades in the water seems like a rude intrusion in the domain of the sleeping giants around you.

To those who travel on the mountains, whether in England or abroad, the usual advice offered by hill-folk is to start your journey while the day is young, and as soon after dawn as possible. In the Alps and Pyrenees it is advice, proved by the experience of generations born and bred in the mountains, which should never be ignored. Even in the English Lake District, although the distances are comparatively short between places where food and shelter can be obtained, the weather is notoriously capricious, and if caught out on the high fells in a violent storm about dusk, the traveller may easily regret that he has not allowed a sufficient margin of daylight to secure his retreat to the nearest valley.

Although it is only about two hours' walk to the summit of Helvellyn from Patterdale, choose the early morning for the climb. You may never meet a soul during the ascent unless it be a shepherd with his dog searching for a missing ewe and her lamb, and on the summit there will be time to identify all the well-known heights before the holiday crowds arrive. The direct route on foot from Patterdale to Grasmere is by Grisedale Hause, and if this track were taken as far as Grisedale Tarn it would afford fine views of Nethermost Cove encircled by formidable looking crags. Helvellyn could then be approached by the path from the tarn over Dollywaggon Pike. But the more exciting and direct ascent is to climb to Striding Edge from near the foot of Grisedale, for then, after you have passed the little gate at the eastern end of Striding Edge, you will get the final thrill without danger of a real mountain track up to the summit of Helvellyn. On the northern side of Red Tarn is an almost similar and characteristic steep climb along Swirrel Edge, and this can be quite exhilarating on a stormy day with a heavy pack on your back. But from Striding Edge there is a better view across Grisedale Forest, exposing the more precipitous escarpment of the Fairfield range and the impressive shape of St. Sunday Crag. Looking eastward appears the long silhouette of the High Street fells already traversed, fading away to the distant lower fells towards Penrith.

From the summit of Helvellyn towards the west opens up the grandest prospect of all, for nearly all the western mountains and high fells of Cumberland stand arrayed in majestic groups. Below you, but invisible, is Thirlmere, and on the other side of this valley the Armboth Fells and Ullscarf stand up as a strong natural barrier guarding the high mountains beyond. Like some primæval rock-god Great Gable raises his domical-shaped head. On his right is the great bulky form of Pillar Fell and, due west from our view-point, the high fells which divide Ennerdale and Buttermere—High Stile and Red Pike. Scafell Pikes and Bowfell present an impressive group to the left of Gable, and still farther towards the south the unmistakable outline of Crinkle Crags carried the eye southward to the Coniston heights. To the north, Skiddaw and Saddleback, in splendid isolation, point the direction for the resumption of the day's tramp. If you are reluctant to leave the tops so early in the day, and wish to explore the lonely tract of country beyond Saddleback to-morrow, your route would lie due north from Helvellyn along the ridge to Stybarrow Dodd and Great Dodd and so to Threlkeld. There are several advantages in this choice, for the sun behind you spreads out a coloured landscape for your delight the whole way and enhances the lovely views down to Ullswater and Thirlmere. This way takes you across the summit of Sticks Pass just where the pony track climbs over the col from the foot of Thirlmere to the Glenridding valley. Another path leads off the fell to the old coaching inn at Thirlspot on the main road.

Our happiest memories of the panorama from Helvellyn have been not in the glare of a midday sun but on summer's evenings when all is peace, and the mountains of the west, mysterious in their thin veil of bluish-purple haze, have drawn us like a magnet to old haunts at farm or camp in Borrowdale. Should your desires be similar, the alternative routes are following the Wythburn valley (visible as you descend Helvellyn) and over the wet top of Greenup, down Greenup Gill towards the tiny village of Stonethwaite ; or over the fells by Harrop Tarn and Blea Tarn to one of the loveliest and quietest hamlets of Cumberland—Watendlath. By either route allow sufficient daylight for getting over the top because the path is vague in parts. Some years ago we realized the difficulty of the walk by night from Wythburn to Watendlath. Having walked from Grange in Borrowdale to Bowness-on-Windermere, by Bowfell, Little Langdale, Skelwith, and the Ferry, we started to return the following day by a different route. In the carefree spirit of youth we left Windermere at noon, and going by Troutbeck and Caudale Moor reached Patterdale for an early dinner, afterwards proceeding over Striding Edge and Helvellyn to call at the Nag's Head, Wythburn.[1] The deepening shadows had blacked out the Armboth Fells, and only the light of hundreds of tiny glow-worms illumined the rough track up the fell-side to Harrop Tarn. From there on, by ill-luck, we lost direction without compass and walked in circles in the brief darkness of a summer's night over ground familiar in daylight, until, with the first streaks of dawn, we arrived at Watendlath and so over Grange Fell to our camp by the Derwent.

To see the dawn from the low fells above Watendlath

[1] The " Nag's Head " has been closed by the Manchester Corporation.

is something not easily forgotten. As the sun rises above the long Helvellyn range all the big fells which encompass the head of Borrowdale appear with renewed strength of outline and warmth of colouring. Little groups of Herdwicks, with the dew sparkling wet on their backs, move from the shelter of peat-hole or fence-wall to their meagre patches of grazing amidst the rocks and heather. Below, towards the north-west, the silvery waters of Bassenthwaite and Derwentwater are seen through the early morning film of mist. Watendlath Tarn, guarded by its single group of dark firs, and the ancient white-washed farm, still slumber in the sheltered bosom of the fells.

From High Seat, above Watendlath, there is a splendid prospect of the Helvellyn Range. To the south the rocky fortresses of Allen Crags, Esk Pike, Bowfell, Crinkle Crags, stand out in bold silhouette. Scafell Pikes and their outlier Lingmell are clearly visible, then, following round clockwise on the horizon come Gable and Kirk Fell, Pillar, High Stile, Dale Head, Hindscarth, and Robinson, and lastly, the boldly-rounded shoulders and summits of the Grassmoor group. There is probably no better short fell-walk for such a panorama of Lakeland hills than the one from Rosthwaite and Watendlath to Keswick over the tops of High Seat and Bleaberry Fell. Here, too, one can well appreciate the intimate connection between geological structure and the shapes and surfaces of the high fells—the rugged and dramatic outlines of the volcanic rocks to the south-west and the gentler contours of the slate mountains to the north and north-west.

3. SKIDDAW AND SADDLEBACK (BLENCATHRA)

In a long day's walk you may climb both Skiddaw and Saddleback, and see something of the lonely hinterland of heathery moor and fell known as Skiddaw Forest. A stiff short ascent from either Threlkeld or the village of Scales will take you to the summit of Saddleback. Standing 2847 feet above sea level, it completely dominates the valley of the Glenderamackin. As a feature of the landscape, there is something peculiarly impressive in the shape and bulk of this great slate mountain when seen from certain viewpoints, particularly looking northward as you leave the lovely Vale of St. John, or from the Penrith road between Keswick and Troutbeck ; and again, as you view it from the " Druid's Circle " on the high ground west of the Naddle Beck.

The south-eastern slopes of the mountain are scooped out by glacial action and a series of becks. The grandest of these natural amphitheatres is filled by Scales Tarn which helps to feed the infant river Glenderamackin. It is past this tarn, by the track from Scales, where you will find the most thrilling approach to the summit along Sharp Edge—a rocky ridge somewhat similar to Striding Edge on Helvellyn although of different geological formation. Having followed this Edge with Scales Tarn immediately below you, a detour along the top to the north-east would enable you to look over the Crags of Bannerdale down to Mungrisdale and get a glimpse of the distant Pennines. From the summit of Saddleback, there lies before you the wide expanse of moorland and fell, forming the gathering ground for the river Caldew, and in the midst of the heather in Skiddaw Forest one lonely dwelling (Skiddaw House). Southward is the grand prospect of the Helvellyn range, seen " end on," and of Thirlmere at the southern end of St. John's Vale.

If you have made an early start, and Skiddaw challenges you across the valley, there is the Glenderaterra Beck just below you for the midday halt and bathe. As you walk south-west down the broad shoulder of the fell past Knowe Crags, you will eventually meet a cart track leading along the contours and parallel with the beck. This well-marked route leads up the valley past the old Blencathra Lead Mine. Here either of the alternative climbs may be taken to Skiddaw. The southern route entails crossing the Glenderaterra Beck, and then by picking up another track you may follow round the southern slopes of Lonscale Fell, cross the White Beck, and arrive on what is virtually a mountain " highway " to the top of Skiddaw. Compared with the stimulating eastern approaches to Saddleback or Helvellyn this is dull going, but a welcome slow ascent for weary limbs on a hot afternoon. Moreover, there is good reason to loiter. Below you, to the south, the glistening mirror of Derwentwater reflects the purple shadows of clouds as they disentangle themselves from the tops of the hills at the head of Borrowdale and sweep northwards over the lake. To the south-west there is a magnificent long-range view of all the high fells between the Buttermere valley and the Derwent. The green Vale of Newlands leads the eye upwards to Dale Head, Hindscarth, and Robinson ; similarly Coledale focuses on the greater heights of Sail and Grassmoor. All these great slate hills have their ice-riven crags on their northerly sides and therefore they appear more impressive when seen from Skiddaw than from any other view-point.

The immense landscape seen from Skiddaw is more arrestingly revealed if the broad summit is directly approached by a less frequented route from Skiddaw House. Then, as you breast the rounded top of the mountain, you can gaze far northwards beyond Bassenthwaite Lake and across the silvery waters of the Solway Firth to the distant blue hills of Scotland, and you see a great tract of country which includes the fertile lowlands of Cumberland. As you descend southward across Carl Side to Millbeck and Crosthwaite, while the shadows lengthen across the Borrowdale Fells, even Causey Pike and Cat Bells, guarding the quiet Vale of Newlands, seem to attain the stature of mountains when seen against the after-glow in the western sky.

4. THE GRASSMOOR-HINDSCARTH GROUP

Two days can be well spent on the two groups of high slate fells enclosed by Whinlatter Pass, Crummock, Honister, and Borrowdale. Starting from Braithwaite, where you may have arrived after your descent from Skiddaw, you can get straight away on the northern fell-side of Coledale and climb up steadily to Grisedale Pike (2593). As you approach the summit the views looking back will bring reward, for across the Vale of Keswick Skiddaw appears regal and splendid on his wide spreading throne. The Crags fall sharply on the

THE NORTHERN VIEW FROM SCAFELL PIKE TO SKIDDAW

northern side of the track to Hobearton Pike. Here you seem to stand on a northern outpost of the mountains, as the green Vale of Lorton opens up the views to the north-west towards Cockermouth and the coastal plain. Whiteside exposes the bones of its southern flank above Gaskill Gill, and these rocky outcrops frame the view looking down to the still waters of Crummock. Unless you intend following the track on the northern side of Whiteside down to Brackenthwaite and Loweswater village, turn southwards to the col (Coledale Pass). So you will get a fine oblique view of the northern crags of Grassmoor, of Eel Crag, and Sail. From the summit of Grassmoor, look southward, and there with the whole of their precipitous crags exposed is the magnificent range of volcanic hills which dominate Buttermere—Red Pike, High Stile, and High Crag. Beyond these is Pillar and, to the south-east, Kirk Fell and its neighbouring heights composed in the distant skyline of the picture.

There is a quick run down the smooth slopes of Grassmoor to Crummock, if you wish, or down the southern shoulder of the fell to Buttermere. More interesting would be the jolly walk along the spine of Sail and Scar Crags to Causey Pike where carpets of bilberries will refresh you during the descent to Little Town. The picture of Newlands church in its perfect frame of trees, and the cluster of white-washed farms, make this hamlet a very lovable place. There could be no pleasanter way of finishing the day's walk than by crossing over the lower fells to Borrowdale where a track runs between Cat Bells and Maiden Moor and so down to Grange. What could be more restful than an evening bathe in the Derwent, and then, from that lovely old bridge at Grange, watching the lazy fat trout in the deep pool beneath the arches. Above you, soaring high over the top of Scawdel Fell, a family of buzzards make great interlacing spirals, and keep watch over the "jaws of Borrowdale." A heron with slow flapping wings comes low overhead and disappears for his evening meal by the fringe of Derwentwater.

We shall return later to this lovely valley, either in the early morning or evening when noisy traffic does not violate its peace, but Grange is a good place from which to begin your next walk along the fell-tops to Buttermere. If you take the track from Manesty to Newlands (by which you arrived yesterday) it will put you on the ridge, and so, turning southwards, you can walk close to the western crags of Maiden Moor and parallel to Eel Crags which tower above the head of Newlands. From Scawdel Fell, and as you descend to Lobstone Band, there are attractive glimpses of the green pastures by Rosthwaite and a vista along the Stonethwaite valley guarded by the rocky bastions of Bull Crag and Eagle Crag. From Lobstone Band, if your immediate objective were shelter in Borrowdale, there is the direct descent by the quarrymen's track to Rosthwaite, or back to Grange under the shadow of Castle Crag; as third choice, follow round the eastern slopes of High Scawdel until you strike the Toll road above Seatoller.

But if you intend to reach Buttermere on the fell-tops, cross the head of the Newlands Beck at Dale Head Tarn and so climb up directly to the sheep fence on the ridge. Hereabouts is to be noted the junction of volcanic rock with slaty outcrops, and there are superb views to north and south as you follow the ridge between the summit of Dale Head and the big hollow cairn on Hindscarth. There you command the views down Little Dale and Newlands to Skiddaw. Across Newlands from Hindscarth is exposed to view the long eastern escarpment of Eel Crags and Maiden Moor. The rounded weather-beaten top of Hindscarth, its friable slates outcropping and speckled here and there with splashes of white rock, ends abruptly at the cairn overlooking Little Dale ; similarly your next summit—Robinson—dominates Keskadale and the pass over Buttermere Hause. By turning southward on the Buttermere slopes of Robinson, you see and realize the great scale of the crags below Fleetwith Pike, and appreciate the difficulties and risk of mining the green slates from the Honister Quarries. These are among the finest roofing slates that Britain can produce, and it may be noted that they come from the igneous rock formations and not from the so-called slate fells as we might expect.

On the way down to Buttermere village across the Moss the lovely trinity of lakes—Buttermere, Crummock, and Loweswater—lie before you ; Loweswater in its quiet and almost pastoral setting ; Crummock Water under the warm shadows of Mellbreak ; Buttermere still more closely enfolded by the high fells on three sides. By whichever lake you choose to spend your night, you will hear the everlasting music of mountain streams and be able to watch the changing colours of the dale head when the setting sun turns the grey battlements of the " Haystacks " and Fleetwith Pike into a golden red.

5. THE SCAFELL REGION

In the last section of this chapter we have included the whole of the high fells on the western side of a line drawn through Coniston-Grasmere-Easedale-Greenup-Honister to Buttermere. This region forms a convenient geographical unit which can be explored at leisure from the dales that radiate from the central watershed of the Scafell-Gable group. Here, too, is manifest the effects of those stupendous earth movements which, in a remote age millions of years ago, forced upwards the volcanic rocks and then denuded them of their overlying formations, leaving their exposed summits to the repeated assaults of glaciers and tempests for countless centuries before man set foot on the mountains of Cumbria. When standing on Great Gable, or when walking northward along Upper Eskdale towards the great basin enclosed by the Scafell-Bowfell range of mountains, we can appreciate the terrific convulsions which produced such a superb climax to the whole region of dales and fells. From whatever dale you approach the central massif, and even when this is viewed at long range, it is difficult to imagine a more impressive group worthy of forming the heart of Lakeland. Rising abruptly from the valley floors, which are but little above sea-level, and with scale and height so often enhanced by a veil of mist and rain, these rugged Cumbrian fells have all the characteristics of Alps in miniature.

BUTTERMERE AND HIGH CRAG

In the previous section we left the reader at Buttermere after a walk over the high slate fells of the northwest, but from now on to the end of this chapter we return to the volcanic rocks, beginning with those hills which form the southern frame to the Buttermere Valley. When clouds hang low on the high fells there is a delightful circular walk from Buttermere which takes you into the district of pink granophyre (*See* Chapter I., p. 20). A track crosses the moors from Crummock by Floutern Tarn to the foot of Ennerdale Water, where the Angler's Inn will surely beguile you, for it enjoys an enviable position right on the edge of the lake, looking straight up the valley with its splendid background of high fells. If you follow the rough road by the lake shore and so up the dale past Gillerthwaite, you will arrive at the little Youth Hostel—once a shepherd's cabin—at the foot of Black Sail which is the pass to Wasdale. A short climb over Scarth Gap will bring you again in sight of Gatesgarth Farm at the head of Buttermere. When visibility is good, there is the much more stimulating experience of the walk along the tops of Red Pike, High Stile, and High Crag. Red Pike may be climbed from Buttermere by the track leading up from Scale Beck which, in a series of cascades and at least one good waterfall (Scale Force), leaps down the mountain-side towards Crummock. Alternatively, you may take the route which begins at the foot of Sour Milk Gill and zig-zags up the fell past Bleaberry Tarn to the "saddle" of Red Pike.

Anywhere along this fine ridge you can look out from rocky pinnacles above exciting precipices. Far below in this enchanting valley are the two lakes, and from the tiny village of Buttermere a thin ribbon of road can be seen winding its way over Buttermere Hause through the Derwent fells to the Newlands valley. By following the narrow ridge over High Crag you will join the pass over Scarth Gap and can then drop down either to Gatesgarth or the head of Ennerdale. If only half your day is spent, and you are content with a humble lodging in the heart of the mountains, get rid of your pack at the Ennerdale Youth Hostel, then climb the fell to the Haystacks and follow the well-cairned track over Brandreth to Green Gable. Here, once again, you are in view of the head of Borrowdale with the bold form of Base Brown guarding Gillercombe. Then, when evening has freed the summits of their noon-tide tourists, you may climb the last steep pitch to pay your homage in silence to the noble head of Great Gable. The whole of the Scafell range of peaks and crags faces you across the Lingmell valley, their summits appearing clear and sharp as an etcher's line above the wisps of cloud which, as they float up Wasdale, strike and seem to recoil against the imperishable breastplates of the mountains. An immense panorama of mountain landscape is before you for selection as you will. It is sufficient to say that in no other place is one more conscious of the superb strength and character of these Cumbrian fells, especially Scafell, as on the summit of Gable, nor can one fail to realize the immensity of those mysterious, overpowering forces which have through countless ages fashioned and revealed Nature in her grandest mood. Here on Gable you may overlook the hub of the gigantic wheel, of which the long ridges in the heart of Lakeland form the spokes and the radiating dales or lakes are the spaces. One of these is Wasdale, where the long black line of screes fall steeply to the lake and frame the view of the coastal plain and sea beyond. As you descend from Gable to Beck Head for your last steep climb to the dual summits of Kirk Fell, you may be feeling the full force of the salt-laden winds from the Atlantic, but Kirk Fell gives you fine views of the crags of Steeple and the head of Mosedale, and there is only a short, rough scramble down to Black Sail. The track then leads you straight to the tiny Ennerdale Hostel which stands alone and unintrusive in this remote dale-head—the cradle of a mountain stream.

One of the reasons for spending a night in this lonely valley amidst the great moraines left by the ice-age is that nowhere else in the district can you sleep dry and warm in a simple shelter so near to the heart of the Lakeland mountains. Except for the recent enclosures of the Forestry Commission, the character of the primæval landscape is typical of many other Cumbrian dale-heads where the rivers have their source. Before retiring to your bed, in what was once a shepherd's refuge, you might cool your sun-scorched limbs nearby in the purest of mountain waters distilled from the clouds broken on the Gable, and if the night be clear and moonlit, the immense black shapes of the Pillar Fell and Kirk Fell will appear as mountain gods guarding the ancient secrets of their haunted valley. It needs little imagination to picture the ghosts of former dales-folk moving slowly with laden pack-horse cavalcade by the rough tracks over Black Sail and Scarth Gap, or of old quarrymen laboriously making their way with sledges along " Moses Sledgait " under the northern crags of Great Gable to Wasdale. Even the old legend of the " girt dog of Ennerd'l," an immense animal which roamed the fells and ravaged the flocks, then seems a credible story connected with these parts. Pillar Fell may appear less formidable on a fine morning, and here at the Youth Hostel you are well placed for the climb by Black Sail and Looking Stead to the summits of Pillar (2927), Steeple, and Haycock, or you may take the more exciting " high-level route " marked by cairns and used by rock-climbers from Looking Stead to the base of the Pillar Rock. From Steeple and Haycock there are wide prospects to the north-west of the Ennerdale and Loweswater Fells as well as across the coastal plain to the Irish Sea. To the south of you lies the unfrequented Copeland Forest, and Wastwater backed by its long line of inhospitable screes.

If Wasdale Head is your objective for the night there is a choice of routes, either from Steeple along the narrow ridge and shoulder of Wasdale Red Pike [1] above the Crags, or from Windy Gap down to Mosedale. The descent to Ennerdale Lake would take you too far from the Scafell Group. Wasdale Head is a place which, sooner or later, the stranger will visit, even although he may not be an enthusiastic rock-climber, for here is the long-established centre of the Fell and Rock Climbing Club. Yet our choice would be to pass on over the Stee to Borrowdale, and so get a

[1] Not to be confused with the Buttermere Red Pike.

GLARAMARA, SCAFELL, AND GREAT GABLE FROM ABOVE ROSTHWAITE

fine close-up view of the Napes Pinnacle on Gable while climbing the pass to Sty Head and before ending our day in one of the best-known Cumberland farm-houses at Seatoller. From Pillar Fell an equally attractive route is by Black Sail, then up the green tongue at the head of Ennerdale, and so over Grey Knotts and Steed Fell to Seatoller. This way you avoid any road walking down Borrowdale or Honister Pass. Seatoller, in spite of the Honister traffic, is still a good place from which to wander among the Borrowdale Fells. Glaramara, for example, that fine mass of knobbly volcanic rock is a noble fell which dominates Borrowdale and affords entrancing views of the valley and surrounding fells. From it, too, you may walk over the summit of Allen Crags to Esk Hause and then descend by Sty Head or Grain Gill, while high up the fell-side in Comb Gill there are caves to entice the inquisitive rambler, and the flora of bogs and mire !

So much has already been written on Scafell Pikes, the goal of all tourists and rock-climbers, that we need not add more than brief notes. From Gable you see the whole of the Scafell Range, but only by traversing its hoary weather-beaten summits will you realize the true nature and scale of its mountain sculpture. There are approaches from Wasdale and Borrowdale *via* Sty Head, from Borrowdale by Grain Gill (the direct ascent to Esk Hause), and from Langdale *via* Rossett Gill ; and Esk Hause is, as it were, the Picca-dilly Circus of these walkers' highways on the big fells. The most lovely and inspiring approach is from Upper Eskdale where the mountains form such a superb natural amphitheatre. From the northern end of the Scafell range, where the Great End buttresses overlook Sprinkling Tarn, to Horn Crag at the southern end of Sca Fell itself it is nearly three miles, but " the Pikes " are separated from Sca Fell by the chasm of Mickledore which offers a way down either to Eskdale or Wasdale. The majority of tourists from Langdale and Borrowdale climb Scafell Pikes (3210) and return by the same route, but if you wish to pass over the summit of Sca Fell (3162) it means a climb and scramble *via* Mickledore and Lords Rake, as the great rocks of Broad Stand bar any progress to the walker from Mickledore on the Eskdale side. There is, however, a direct ascent to Sca Fell from Eskdale past Cam Spout if you wish.

There is little need for us to attempt a description of the magnificent prospects to be enjoyed on a clear day from there—the noblest of our English mountains. All the southern half of the Lake District spreads out like a map before you, and across the sea the distant outline of the Isle of Man and Scotland are plainly visible. Immediately across Eskdale, Bowfell and Crinkle Crags are seen in a new perspective and lead the eye southward to the Coniston Fells. From the crude stone shelter on Esk Hause (2490), a very short climb will bring you to Esk Pike (2903), and here you look straight down Lang Strath, still one of the most lonely and characteristic dale-heads in Cumberland. Below the eastern crags of Esk Pike, and collecting the melted snow from its gullies, is Angle Tarn, its icy waters feeding the Langstrath Beck. As you follow the high ground from the Pike to Bowfell you are approaching the boundary of Westmorland, for this county claims the whole of Langdale to the summits of Rossett Gill and Stake Pass, also Easdale and the Rotha valley up to the top of Dunmail Raise. It seems an arbitrary boundary until one realizes that these dale-head parishes, and the farms in them, claim their sheep-runs up to the watersheds. From Bowfell a track will take you down " The Band " to Stool End Farm, or by the cascades of Hell Gill into Oxendale. If you like to follow along the knobbly summits of Crinkle Crags, you will have the pleasure of that long enfilading view down the whole of Dunnerdale and ultimately descend to the summit of Wrynose Pass, where the three Lakeland counties join hands at " Three Shire Stone." Here you are once more on the Roman route from Penrith to the sea which we followed at High Street, while above you the pyramid-shaped Pike o' Blisco looks down on the green pastures of Langdale.

So we may pass from Wrynose to the last group of fells above Coniston, which present such a fine silhouette when seen from the head of Windermere. Here, too, we are still among the old volcanic rocks. From Wrynose Pass you might walk along the spine of these hills to the Old Man, making a detour to Wetherlam. Much more interesting is the approach from Eskdale to Dow Crag overlooking Goats Water and northward to Brim Fell, Wetherlam, and on to Little Langdale. By this route you avoid direct contact with the untidy remains of old copper workings near Coniston, and yet enjoy the charm of distant views across the beautiful lowland country of Furness.

In such a brief sketch of a tour on foot among the high fells we have only presumed to indicate to the reader the general character of the country which forms the "Heart of the Lake District," and particularly those parts which can only be traversed on foot. In the next chapter we can explore the dales. You may spend weeks, walking and climbing, within a three-mile radius of Esk Hause, and still experience fresh revelations of beauty. Under the ever-changing conditions of brilliant sunshine, threatening clouds and misty rain, the old familiar views and colouring are transformed or obliterated, and reappear in a new and unsuspected grandeur. There are folk, just as there were among the eighteenth-century writers, who are repelled, or even afraid, in seeing Nature in her wilder moods, but they would instantly respond to the more sophisticated pastoral beauty of a downland landscape. Yet the poetry of earth is as clearly manifest in romantic mountain scenery as in the restful classic lines of the East Anglian landscape or the gentle contouring of chalk downs. There is, too, some deep-rooted instinct in man which stimulates him to match his strength against Nature in her wildest moods. Little wonder that from the large cities, every year, come increasing numbers of enthusiastic walkers to our Lakeland fells, for there, whatever the weather may promise, lies freedom to roam and beauty not denied to the poorest. But the sanctity of the mountain gods is already in danger of assault. The procession of cars over the new motor road at Honister has only recently shattered the peace of one valley. The proposed motor highway from Borrowdale to

Wasdale threatens to penetrate the last stronghold of those who walk the high fells, unless the insensibility and folly of those responsible for this project is exposed to ridicule by all lovers of the mountains. If once the noise of explosive exhausts reverberates under Glaramara, by Sty Head Tarn, and, indeed, under the very feet of Great Gable, all the romance and mystery of these high places will have vanished.

III

THE LAKES AND DALES (*WESTERN AREA*)

I. DUNNERDALE

For convenience of map reference and touring we have grouped together in this chapter all the dales which have their outlets in the western half of the Lake District. As we left the reader in the previous chapter in the neighbourhood of Wrynose Pass, it is a good starting-point to explore Dunnerdale.

In nearly all Lakeland valleys the scenery can be best appreciated by travelling towards the dale-head, *i.e.* up the valley so that there is a gradual crescendo of interest as one approaches the central massifs. Dunnerdale may be taken as an exception to the rule, for it is the middle reaches of the river which are the most exciting, and the grand expanse of sands in the estuary affords much finer prospects than Wrynose Bottom at the dale-head. As you go down the pass from the " Three Shire Stone " you are again following the footsteps of the Legionaries on their way over Hard Knott to the Roman Camp which commands Eskdale. Numerous little becks made " water-splashes " across the rough road in Wrynose Bottom, and in winter when these are charged with the melting snow from the high Seathwaite Fells they rapidly scour great channels across the road on their way to swell the waters of Duddon. At Cockley Beck, near the point where the Roman road crossed the Moasdale Beck to Hard Knott, stands the highest farm at the dale-head—one of those satisfactory little groups of unpretentious buildings with low-pitched, green-slated roofs which give the right human scale to a Lakeland valley. This farm, like another dale-head farm in Langdale, is fortunately in the hands of the National Trust.

As the river and road turn southward the valley floor widens, and is punctuated only by Castle How—a miniature outlier of the fell facing the Youth Hostel at Dale Head. Perhaps the most lasting impression of this upper section of Dunnerdale is made by the finely shaped Harter Fell, whose summit seems to stand unchallenged between Esk and Duddon. The country between these two dales is now in the hands of the Forestry Commissioners, and it extends far northward through Moasdale to Esk Hause. The native deciduous trees, which here and there exist precariously in sheltered places near the becks and add interest to the fell-sides, will soon be obliterated by a blanket of dull green conifers unless the greatest skill is exercised in making the new plantations harmonize with the contours and native woodlands of the dale. A precious quality of the dale-heads in the Lake District is their open appearance with bare fell-sides falling uninterrupted to the valley floor, but the whole character of the landscape must inevitably change when the varied greens of upland pasture, the golden brown of bracken, and patches of heather, are submerged and killed under a dense plantation of sombre pine trees where no other form of life can exist.

Just above Birks Bridge—one of those simple stone-arched structures which grace many a northern dale—the valley narrows and the Duddon has here carved out its lovely gorge, where the crystal-clear water runs in a channel cleft deep between lichen-covered rocks, here and there overhung with the delicate foliage of mountain-ash and birch. Below Birks Bridge there is all the pleasure and freedom of following an unfenced road with enchanting views down the dale, and as the road sweeps upwards and over a shoulder of the fell there comes into view the valley of the Tarn Beck—a tributary stream, "the fairest, softest, liveliest of them all." Here, in this little dale, lies Seathwaite church, and hereabouts also the fell track from Eskdale to Coniston by Walna Scar crosses Dunnerdale. It is a most useful cross-country route which climbs over Birker Moor and comes into Dunnerdale at Grass Gars alongside another rollicking tributary of the Duddon.

From Dunnerdale Brig, where the road crosses to the Cumberland side of the river, down to Ulpha, the dale loses its wild character, but it has all the beauty of a lowland stream as it winds its course through the wooded hillsides to its well-guarded approach at Duddon Bridge. Then, as it were with a fine gesture, the river seems suddenly to burst from its discreetly hidden vale, and gives us the grand prospect of

> "Majestic Duddon, over smooth flat sands
> Gliding in silence with unfettered sweep"

as it mingles with tidal waters, the haunt of almost every species of bird which love to feed in the margins of this wide estuary.

2. ESKDALE AND MITERDALE

Those who wish to walk from the foot of Dunnerdale to Eskdale can avoid the main coastal road which runs from Broughton-in-Furness through Bootle to Ravenglass, as there are several breezy and attractive ways over the heather-clad moors. You may cut across country by footpath from Duddon Bridge to the prehistoric stone circle on Swinside and there join a moorland track over Stoneside Hill ; and from there onwards till you gain the motor road at Bridge End you will have before you a fine view of the coast and the ancient harbour of Ravenglass—the terminus of the Roman route from the head of Windermere. Two other tracks to Eskdale also afford splendid prospects of sea and the high fells : one from Ulpha passing just north of Whitfell to Bridge End : the other from Ulpha over Black Moor to Boot. The latter route brings you close to Devoke Water—that little-known lake, not much bigger than a tarn, which lies high on the fringe of the Eskdale granite.

To realize fully the beauty of Eskdale you should travel up the valley from the sea to Esk Hause where the river is born, for so you will be able to appreciate the harmonious changes of scene as the valley is gradually confined by the high fells on both sides ; and having passed the hospitable enclosures of Brotherelkeld—the highest farm in the valley—the pastoral beauty of Mid-Eskdale is replaced by a primitive wildness and grandeur which culminates with a superb climax in a mountain amphitheatre. There is no visible outlet to the dale-head—uncomparably the finest termination of any Lakeland valley by reason of the fact that all the highest of the volcanic mountains form a great horseshoe-shaped barrier around the head of the dale, giving it a unity of form unequalled anywhere in this region. It is true that Wasdale and Ennerdale are both enhanced by the huge shape of Great Gable standing as a focal point to each dale-head, and in Langdale the Pikes close the vista from many view-points in this valley ; yet in all three cases there is the lack of a continuous mountain barrier such as is seen at the head of Eskdale, which is a sufficiently high background to dominate both Upper Eskdale and its tributary valley of the Lingcove Beck.

The outstanding feature of Lower Eskdale is Muncaster Fell, a commanding ridge of rough pinkish granite clothed with bracken, which stands up some 750 feet above the estuary and separates Miterdale from the marshes of the Esk. Along the southern slopes of the fell there is a fine route for walkers from Muncaster Castle Park towards Eskdale Green and the valley road to Boot ; or, if you choose to avoid the road, cross the river near Eskdale Green, and so use a more interesting track on the left bank leading to Dalegarth Hall where Mid-Eskdale may be said to begin. There is, of course, that odd little " toy-railway " which meanders up the valley of the Mite from Ravenglass on the north side of Muncaster Fell and serves (very infrequently) both Eskdale Green and Boot, where it expires ; and as this is the nearest rail approach to Wasdale Head, therefore beyond Boot it means a moorland walk up the valley of the Whillan Beck and by the track past Burnmoor Tarn to the head of Wastwater.

Mid-Eskdale in many ways rivals the beauty of Borrowdale and, happily, it is more free from the invasions of tourist traffic. You may follow the stream on either bank as it winds its lovely course past high banks and little woodlands of great charm. Always in sight there is Harter Fell—the finely contoured hill separating Esk from Duddon : then comes the jolly group of typical Cumbrian buildings at Brotherelkeld (Butterilket), set amidst trees and level green pastures. Here comes in the pass over Hard Knott from Langdale and Wrynose, and over the high pastures of the surrounding fells roam the Herdwick flocks of Brotherelkeld. It is of interest to climb up the fell-side to Hardknott Castle—the Roman camp which commands the dale and the last stage of the invaders' march to Ravenglass Harbour. There are but scanty remains of the Legion's occupation in the second century A.D., but the earthen ramparts, foundations, and level parade ground can be identified, and there is a glorious view across bracken-covered fell-sides to Upper Eskdale and its background of Scafell. Yew Crags and Heron Crags enclose the valley above Brotherelkeld, and the track runs close to the river where it approaches Esk Falls and the old pack-horse bridge at the foot of Lingrove Beck.

It may be noted that the whole of Upper Eskdale

YEWBARROW, GREAT GABLE AND LINGMELL FROM WAST WATER

(east of the river) up to the summits of Esk Hause, Bow Fell, and Crinkle Crags, which embrace the Lingcove valley, is now owned by the Forestry Commissioners, but fortunately almost the whole of the area above Brotherelkeld will not be planted, nor, indeed, should any of the grand characteristics of this supremely beautiful valley be disfigured by the incongruous and highly artificial lines of conifer forests. Eskdale is unique in the landscape of English valleys. It approaches the scale and grandeur of many valleys in the Pyrenees, and even although the dale-head does not terminate in a vast vertical rampart of rock such as the Cirque de Gavarnie, it has all those qualities of plan and shape, unity of colour and form, and a grand climax seldom seen in valley scenery. As you pass upwards into the dale-head and finally arrive at the broad amphitheatre of volcanic fells, the perfect harmony, the wild beauty, and loneliness of a primitive landscape leaves an impression never forgotten. Wordsworth might fittingly have applied to the Esk those lines from the Duddon sonnets, for the infant stream starts its adventurous life over 2000 feet up at the very heart of the central massif of Cumbria.

> " Child of the clouds ! remote from every taint
> Of sordid industry thy lot is cast."

3. WASDALE

After reading our notes on Eskdale, the stranger to these parts might conclude that there is no passage from this valley-head into Wasdale. There are, in fact, three well-known routes over the top, and others for the more enterprising fell-walker ; but in all cases the going is fairly strenuous. The line of least resistance is *via* Esk Hause which you gain by ascending the green tongue on the west side of, and well above, the river, and so by the Hause (2490) to Sty Head and Wasdale Head. The other routes entail climbing over the Scafell Range, either over Sca Fell itself *via* Cam Spout, or over Mickledore—the chasm between the Pikes and Sca Fell. But if you should wish to enter Wasdale at its lower end there is the upland road from Eskdale Green across Miterdale to Santon Bridge, or a higher track over Irton Fell direct to Wasdale ; better still, to take the latter and deviate right from the fell track towards the bridge over the Irt at the foot of Wastwater. Then you will have the enfilading view along the screes, and be able to see or explore Hawl Gill before you leave the Eskdale granite.

While walking up the dale by the lake-side road, opposite the steep pitch of the screes which sweep down from Whin Rigg unchecked, black, and sinister, one can well believe that Wastwater is over 250 feet deep and that at some remote age this valley, hemmed in by the high fells of hard igneous rock, was scooped out by glaciers leaving the lake bottom below present sea-level. The river Irt, draining the lake, follows a tortuous course down the valley to join the same estuary as the Esk by Ravenglass, and on its way gathers the waters of a long tributary from Blengdale. Between the latter and Mosedale is Copeland Forest—a wild stretch of fell country bisected by the valley of the Nether Beck which rises far up the slopes of Scoatfell and above Scoat Tarn. Another beck almost isolates Yewbarrow from the shoulders of the Scoatfell-Red Pike range, so that it is Yewbarrow which makes such a fine frame to Wasdale Head where the valley attains real grandeur. Lingmell, with its sturdy shoulders, seems to support the northern precipices of the great Scafell heights, while Great Gable—really a true gable when seen from the head of the lake—stands proudly, a magnificent climax to the valley view. The valley-head, above its tiny church, is split in two by the southern shoulder of Kirk Fell; Lingmell Beck, pouring down from the gulley under Broad Crag (where under the name of Piers Gill it affords problems for rock climbers), forms the eastern branch of the dale-head, and Mosedale is the western branch. Mosedale is a particularly fine example of a lesser dale-head, terminating abruptly against a horseshoe-shaped barrier of precipitous crags, with Scoatfell at the point of the horse-shoe and Wasdale Red Pike and Pillar Fell at each side.

It is, perhaps, the contrast in the components of the landscape at Wasdale Head which gives so much charm to this Cumberland valley—the great volcanic mountains on all sides, proud and irresistible, soaring upwards, and below them the little flat green meadows, so expressive of man's labours to tame wild Nature, and enclose the tiny patches of greensward with the boulders gathered and broken from the debris of the Ice Age. Moreover, the church, inn, and the few simple dwellings sheltered by a few trees, which together make up this diminutive hamlet, give the welcome human addition to an otherwise primitive landscape.

Three well-known fell tracks connect Wasdale with the neighbouring valleys: one by Burnmoor Tarn to Boot, and in the late summer when the heather is in bloom there is a magnificent splash of colour to cheer the traveller on this route: the second, over Sty Head into Borrowdale or *via* Esk Hause into Langdale: the third, up Mosedale and over Black Sail into Ennerdale.

4. ENNERDALE

As we shall have something to say on the "Fringe of the Lake District" in a later chapter, there is no need here to make that long but interesting journey round the western edge of the fell country in order to approach Ennerdale at its seaward end. Much less than one hour's walking will take you from Mosedale over the Black Sail and put you in the middle of the moraines at the head of Ennerdale mentioned in the previous chapter. There are similar conical mounds of gravel and pulverized rock left by the glaciers also near the top of Greenup Gill above Borrowdale, and they give a fair idea of at least one phase in the making of the lakeland landscape. Ennerdale is unlike all the other valleys of the Lake District—with the possible exception of Long Sleddale—in its long undeviating course from the lake to the dale-head where the river Liza has its source under the northern crags of Great Gable. If you stand anywhere on the high ground between Green Gable and Brandreth there is a magnifi-

LOWESWATER AND CARLING KNOTT

cent view westward extending the full eight and a half miles from the valley-head to the foot of Ennerdale Water, and far beyond this to the Solway Firth. Except for the little stone shelter, which serves as a Youth Hostel at the foot of Black Sail, there is no sign of a building until you reach Gillerthwaite—the old dale-head farm. On the northern side the almost continuous line of steep fell-sides, broken only by Scarth Gap, seem to emphasize the great length and funnel-like appearance of the valley. The enclosures of young conifers recently planted by the Forestry Commissioners have intruded a formal feature on a primitive landscape, otherwise the scene must have remained unchanged for countless centuries, during which the Pillar Rock has stood sentinel over the wildest and loneliest of the Cumberland dales.

To appreciate the real majesty of the Pillar Fell and Steeple—those giants which overlook the valley on its southern side—you should view them approaching from the foot of the lake past Bowness Knotts, a rugged outlier of the fell which, like Angling Crag on the southern shore, is thrust forward to form an inner gateway to the valley-head. Or you might skirt the south side of the lake to the footbridge over the Liza at Gillerthwaite and so have before you the grand Red Pike range which separates Ennerdale from Buttermere. Yet, as you walk up the valley, the southern slopes of these great fells do not stir the imagination like the frowning ice-riven precipices of Pillar or the massive bulk of Kirk Fell with its boulder-strewn slopes. Last and pre-eminent is Gable—the climax at the dale-head.

5. BUTTERMERE, CRUMMOCK, AND LOWESWATER

The direct passage from the very top of Ennerdale to Buttermere is over Brandreth and down the Haystacks gullies into Warnscale Bottom. By this route, or again from the summit of Fleetwith Pike which commands Honister, you may enjoy superb views of the whole valley. There are, however, attractive and alternate routes to the Buttermere valley from the north-west, and from Cockermouth up the Vale of Lorton. So you may overcome any difficulties of transport from the foot of Ennerdale or rail-head. If bound for Loweswater from Ennerdale Bridge, where the valley widens and the river Eden begins its great loop round the western fells, you may take your choice of routes to Lamplugh—a pleasant little village, and then skirt the fells by a jolly road which enters the Loweswater valley with an abrupt turn at Fangs. Here the road descends to one of the most charming of the smaller lakes, for Loweswater is much enhanced by the well-wooded hillsides on its southern shore. Just below the lake the village enjoys a lovely site with views southward up three little valleys, and towards Mellbreak—that beautiful fell which stands apart from its neighbours and slopes steeply to the shore of Crummock.

There are really three main divisions of the dale: firstly, the lower reach of the Cocker—from Cockermouth to Brackenthwaite, and known as the Vale of Lorton; secondly, Crummock Water; and lastly, Buttermere, with its dale-head at the top of Honister. Loweswater flows into Crummock, and is really a side appendage—but a very beautiful one—of the main valley. It provides a lateral approach to Crummock from the west just as Gaskill Gill affords a passage through the fells from the east (Coledale Pass), and as the Sail Beck valley offers a route over Buttermere Hause.

The Vale of Lorton is a fitting introduction to the high fells which face you all the way from Cockermouth. It is typical of much of the enclosed undulating country on the fringe of the Lake District, with a quiet pastoral beauty and an intimate charm. At Crummock one is more directly aware of the mountains. High Stile dominates the scene, and on either flank the broad shoulders of Mellbreak and the slopes of Grassmoor close in the dale. Even more so do Rannerdale Knotts, and as you pass round that sharp bend and promontory on the lake shore just below the Knotts there is revealed the lovely view of Buttermere and the mountain background by Gatesgarth. But do not hurry past Crummock, for much as you may be drawn towards the dale-head, there lies to the east the splendid group of high slate fells which centre on Grassmoor: Wandope, Whiteless Pike, and Blake Rigg form the long spine of the fells which points southward to Buttermere. There is a most engaging view of these hills from the little shingle beach by the shores of Crummock near Ling Crag, just where Scale Beck enters the lake from the side of Starling Dodd, bringing down with it the pinkish fragments of Eskdale granite. Here can be seen how much the fine modelling and colour of Rannerdale Knotts contribute to the beauty of Crummock Water. From the boat landing also, looking down the lake, one can appreciate the value of Mellbreak as it gives just that right sense of enclosure to the northward view.

There are very few villages in the whole of the Lake District in such a beautiful position as that at Buttermere. We would avoid it during the tourist season because of traffic in the middle of the day which now disturbs its peace, but in the quiet of the early mornings and evenings it is a place to stay or loiter in. Situated as it is mid-way between the two lakes, it enjoys the views of all the high fells to the north up the valley of the Sail Beck. Better still is that lovely backcloth of mountains across Buttermere—Red Pike, High Stile, and High Crag, with their steepest crags and summits all visible from the valley. Sour Milk Gill pours its white ribbon of cascading water straight down the fell-side from Bleaberry Tarn which lies far up between the breasts of Red Pike and High Stile, and another beck comes down from the " hanging " valley between High Stile and High Crag. The still waters of the lake reflect the mountains and the tall Scotch firs by the shore at Hasness. Finally, when you look up the dale, the view is terminated by the high crags of Fleetwith Pike and the Haystacks which form such an impressive crescent-shaped frame to Warnscale Bottom. This is the visible dale-head when seen from the valley road by Buttermere, because after passing Gatesgarth Farm the valley bends to the left under the foot of Fleetwith, and, as it narrows, so also it becomes wilder with all the boulder-strewn slopes and other characteristics of true mountain scenery. The summit of Honister Pass is crowned by the buildings and equipment of the famous slate quarries, which are, in fact, mines, for these fine roofing slates are cut from the volcanic rock right in the heart of Honister Crag—a natural fortress commanding the approach to Borrowdale from Buttermere.

6. BORROWDALE

We may regret that the day is past when only one or two four-horse coaches rolled lazily up Borrowdale on the way over Honister to Buttermere, and that now, during the summer holidays, there is a constant procession of cars and motor buses; yet we have not been deprived of the glories of this supremely beautiful valley, and in our opinion it is still the best and most conveniently situated centre for walking in the western half of the Lake District. Those who return to Borrowdale year after year to roam the fells do so with good reason; for within three hours you may walk to the summit of any of the western mountains, while a little longer time brings within walking range both Helvellyn and Saddleback. In its valley scenery, also, Borrowdale has no rival. The lonely and primitive grandeur of Langstrath, of Greenup, and Grain Gill: the emerald clear pools of the Stonethwaite Beck: the milky-white cascades leaping down from the high bowl of Gillercombe where the little Herdwicks find their summer pasture: the still beauty of Watendlath Tarn on a summer's morn: the Derwent winding musically through the lovely woodlands and ravine by Castle Crag—all these and much more make Borrowdale rank very high in any valuation of English scenery. Certainly no other Lakeland valley has a more striking natural gateway to guard its beauty. When approaching from the direction of Keswick, the fringe of low-lying pastures at the head of Derwentwater with the river meandering through them gives just the right foreground to enhance the beauty of Grange and its picturesque double bridge of slender stone arches. Ever since the early days when the Cistercian monks of Furness established here one of their "granges" for sheep-farming, flocks of Herdwicks have made their annual journey from Grange to the "heaf" on the high pastures of the Borrowdale fells. The site of this little village was well selected, as one might expect from the Cistercians (who were also responsible for the establishment of another "grange" at Butterelkeld in Eskdale), for Grange-in-Borrowdale stands at the lowest river crossing safe from floods above the head of Derwentwater, and the highest point from which small boats can navigate to the lake and to Keswick.

Nature has provided a perfect entrance to this lovely valley. The long ridge of Maiden Moor and Scawdel Fell on the western side, and Grange Fell—a superbly modelled outcrop of volcanic rock—on the eastern side together make a strong enclosing frame of hills; and between them Castle Crag stands proudly as if conscious of its age-old privilege as a natural fortress guarding the "jaws of Borrowdale." The road from Grange to Rosthwaite through the "jaws," where it runs close to the river and hemmed in by hanging woods, is one of great beauty. It is a road to loiter on during the hours when there is little traffic, especially in the early summer evenings when the western sun throws shafts of golden light over the crest of Scawdel Fell on to the delicate fresh green foliage of birch and beech by the river banks.

After passing through the "jaws" the valley floor broadens out to form the enclosed green winter pastures and meadows of Rosthwaite farms. Across these runs the Stonethwaite Beck to pay tribute to the Derwent, and it is this little beck—that almost trebles its size in winter—which is such a charming feature of Rosthwaite, a friendly village which has changed but little during the last twenty-five years, although the two inns have been modernized to meet the demands of tourists. To see how Rosthwaite really lives through the long wet days of winter you must leave the main road and visit the old farmhouses on the lane which leads to the Derwent. When the lambs arrive, and a little later when they are strong enough to go to the "Heaf" up Langstrath, the narrow lanes will be crowded and noisy with anxious ewes and bleating offspring, with barking sheep-dogs and all the excitement that denotes an early departure for the high fells.

If you wish to avoid the tourist traffic in Borrowdale and glean something of the character of the valley before it was linked up to the outer world by motor bus, there is the delightful but rough boulder-strewn track from Grange on the west side of the Derwent—an old pack-horse and quarry-sled track which follows the river through the woods under Low Scawdel, and climbs under the western foot of Castle Crag. So it forms a good approach to the Quarries of Lobstone Band, and a high-level terrace route to the Honister Toll road. There are splendid views looking across the level pastures to Rosthwaite to which a track and footbridge over the Derwent gives access; and the high-level route also affords a grand prospect of all the Borrowdale Fells—Rosthwaite Fell separating the Derwent from Langstrath and leading up to the greater heights of Glaramara, and the Stonethwaite valley leading up to Greenup Edge and pointing the direction to Grasmere.

Seatoller has somehow or other managed to preserve its character and hospitality even in spite of the recent construction of a motor road to Buttermere which has robbed both the old coach road and the wooded dell by Hause Gill of their quiet charm. Even the rough cart-track from Seatoller to Seathwaite has been given its unnecessary finish of tar-mac, and the walker must traverse this to gain Sty Head *via* Stockley Bridge. He can, however, take the little track up the fell-side and enjoy the wild beauty of Gillercombe, and so pass the survivors of Wordsworth's ancient yews, "those fraternal Four of Borrowdale."

Seathwaite is a grey and grim little hamlet with the heaviest annual rainfall (150 inches) of any spot in England, but it marks the dale-head and the welcome approach to the complete freedom of the mountains. So, too, does the really typical village of Stonethwaite near Rosthwaite. Here in its well-placed diminutive church is to be placed the pulpit from Mardale church, already demolished and soon to be submerged by order of the Manchester Corporation. Stonethwaite village has all the true character of a Lakeland village, the last with road access before you take to the rough bridle tracks which enter

BORROWDALE, GRANGE FELL AND SKIDDAW

Langstrath. Once more the traveller must rely on his own legs to explore this lovely survival of a primitive Cumbrian dale, so admirably described by Mr. H. H. Symonds in his book, *Walking in the Lake District.* Nature was indeed in her grandest mood when she conceived those impressive rocky bastions—Bull Crag and Eagle Crag—to protect the approach to Langstrath, nor could human skill have contrived more fascinating deep pools to entice the bather than those which have so often delayed our journeys and cooled our limbs after the climb over the Stake Pass from Langdale. The absence of trees, except the gnarled and wind-pruned, ancient ash trees near the foot of the "Stake," seems to emphasize the elemental austere beauty of the fell sides; the great boulders left in the bottoms by the glaciers as they poured down long since from the central massif: overhead on the crags of Glaramara the croak of the ravens and the shrill cry of buzzards: the curious sudden sneeze of the little hardy sheep as they stare suspiciously at the traveller—such are the first impressions which the stranger may receive on his approach through Langstrath to the more cultivated beauty of Borrowdale.

7. DERWENTWATER AND BASSENTHWAITE

We may leave Borrowdale and approach Derwentwater by way of Grange Fell—a lovely possession of the National Trust—which is such a prominent feature in every view from the lake or dale. It is indeed fortunate that this property of the Trust, comprising more than 300 acres, safeguards for all time the beautiful entrance to the valley, including the riverside birches between Grange and the Rosthwaite meadows. On leaving Rosthwaite by the Watendlath track which crosses over the Stonethwaite Beck, the open fell-side is quickly gained, and after passing through the top " intake " you may wander anywhere among the rocks and heather of Grange Fell. This is a mountain in miniature, complete with crags and summits and unexpected gullies, open patches of smooth turf, a variety of heather, and a little valley of its own where a beck splashes down through bracken and groves of thorn and rowan to join the Derwent. A whole day could well be spent enjoying the intimate loveliness of this area which epitomizes the scenery of Borrowdale. From any of its rocky vantage-points the prospects on all sides are tremendous. In the evening especially, when the shadows lengthen under the crags of Maiden Moor and peace descends on the valley, all the high mountains at the dale-head are unified into one great brotherhood by that mysterious purple haze which enhances their height and harmonizes their contrasting shapes and rugged contours.

You may omit to visit the Bowder Stone—that enormous boulder, carefully poised on its narrow base, which seems to fascinate the tourist—but the valley of the Watendlath Beck is one that should not be side-tracked, for it is not only beautiful in itself, but as you descend to Ashness Bridge there are enchanting views across Derwentwater to Skiddaw. The little hamlet of Watendlath, snug and hidden from the outer world by Grange Fell, may have lost some of its loneliness since the writings of Sir Hugh Walpole endowed it with romance, but it is still a fascinating place. Publicity cannot destroy the beauty of its site above the beck and tarn.

Although the main road from Lodore to Keswick has very much to offer to those who are insensitive to traffic, there is no need to follow it, because Falcon Crag and Walla Crag both afford grand views over the lake and its well-wooded islands, and you may visit both summits by fell tracks. There is, too, another delightful alternative. By entering the main road at Ashness Gate, you are within a quarter of a mile of the footpath close to the lake which runs through the National Trust property of Calf Close Bay,[1] and so continues as a right of way near Stable Hill farm to Friar's Crag and the Keswick boat-landings. At Friar's Crag—a lovely promontory of igneous rock adorned with Scotch firs—you are quite close, so geologists tell us, to one of the centres of volcanic activity which millions of years ago laid the foundations of the landscape of Borrowdale. Quite near is Castlehead, which has a curious formation suggestive of the "remains of an extinct volcano," and although only some 530 feet high it offers a good bird's-eye view of Keswick and its surroundings, and fortunately the foreground will remain safeguarded by the National Trust. Of greater interest to the antiquarian is the so-called "Druid's Circle" on Castlerigg—a notable monument in a district not otherwise rich in archæological remains. One authority claims that the stone circle is possibly of Neolithic origin, that the sanctuary may have been added in the Bronze Age, and that this meeting-place

[1] Ordnance Map: "Scarf Close Bay."

was used by the Druids and early Christians under St. Kentigern. It is perhaps the dominating shapes of Skiddaw and Blencathra, looking down on this ancient site which ages ago inspired man to celebrate his most solemn rites in this "ring of great grey stones, a mysterious conclave."

We have diverted the reader from the shores of Derwentwater, and here, in a district so loved and often described by Gray and Keats, by Ruskin and Rawnsley, and a host of other writers, we do not intend to trespass. To realize the ever-changing beauty of this lake you must not only explore its lovely margins and islands by boat, but view it from all the adjoining fells when sun, cloud shadows, and mist endow it with an infinite variety of colour-harmonies. It is perhaps something of an anti-climax, having traversed the attractive old road under Cat Bells, to leave Derwentwater behind and pass Swinside and Braithwaite to the shores of Bassenthwaite. We have now turned our backs to the high fells and are approaching the more sophisticated pastoral scenery of the Vale of Derwent. It has its undoubted charms, and there are moments when one can well imagine Bassenthwaite as a long inlet of the sea, or at least one continuous lagoon-like lake joined to Derwentwater. The western shores, almost straight, make direct contact with the steep-sided and afforested fells, in marked contrast to the serrated margins of the lowland farms on the eastern side of the lake. At the " Pheasant "—one of the most characteristic of the Lakeland inns—we can leave the Vale of Derwent for another occasion.

THE WESTERN FELLS FROM DERWENTWATER

8. THIRLMERE AND THE VALE OF ST. JOHN

In Chapter II. we have already drawn the reader's attention to the superb view of Thirlmere and the Vale of St. John from the southern side of Saddleback. The distance of this vantage-point lends enchantment, because a closer inspection of the lake reveals all the disturbing elements of artificiality inseparable from the work of the efficient water engineers. Even the passage of years has not softened much the hard mechanical precision of dams, culverts, and iron railings which bear the stamp of the office drawing board and the Manchester Corporation. Nobody can wish to deny the supply of pure mountain water to supply the needs of an overgrown and congested city, which recently has also demanded additional supplies from Haweswater, nor could we object to the planting of the fell-sides to conserve the winter rains. Manchester has effectively safeguarded its water supply, and the "Lakeland Landscape" has suffered in consequence. When the original natural lake—which is well depicted by the old topographers—was raised in level, a useful road was made skirting the western side of the lake which provided an interesting alternative route, and afforded better views of the noble breasts of the Helvellyn Range than the old highway past Wythburn and Thirlspot. It was a route good to walk on, even although confined by stone walls and punctuated at intervals by red iron gates. Now the regimented rows of dull green conifers have completely hedged in the traveller on both sides and obscured the scenery of the lake and fells, with the result that the main highway past Wythburn is now much more attractive to the tourist. To add insult to injury the old Nag's Head Inn at Wythburn has been closed, and there is nothing there to detain us except a charming example of a little Cumberland church, a monument of the simple faith of generations of departed dalesmen. Departed also are most of the Herdwick flocks that once roamed over ground now occupied by gloomy fir trees which seem to close every vista in the scenery of Thirlmere. But follow up the valley of the Wyth Burn—the principal feeder of the lake—and once more you will recapture the spirit of the dale, and be able to look back on Helvellyn and the other high fells which form a catchment area of 10,000 acres to fill the glasses and flush the sewers of the grim northern metropolis.

We may pass from the tidy and urbanized landscape of Thirlmere to its outfall along one of the most charming cultivated vales of the Lake District. At Thirlspot there is an old coaching inn which has for long shown a welcome face to the traveller, and up to quite recent times it heard the musical note of the coachman's horn on his daily journey with mails and passengers from Windermere to Keswick. The pastoral beauty of St. John's Vale is enhanced by characteristic farmhouses and cottages cheerfully colour-washed or in natural local stone which blends so happily with the neighbouring crags and intake walls. There is, too, a spice of romance about this pleasant valley, for is there not the legend of the castellated bastions of St. John's Vale appearing to the royal traveller from the north as a real fortress seen against the setting sun and guarding the passage of the Vale?—and the Castle Rock[1] certainly commands the old highway through the valley to the lake and Dunmail Raise. Yet for those who follow down-stream to Threlkeld it is Saddleback which focuses the eye beyond Threlkeld—an impressive background to every distant view.

About a mile to the north of the inn at Thirlspot the main road to Keswick leaves the vale and climbs over a low col which separates the valleys of the Naddle Beck and St. John's Beck. It is essentially a motorists' route with its wide sweeping curves, but the more leisurely traveller will follow the narrow and more picturesque road through the vale. At the point where these two roads join, the old pony track climbs up the fellside to Sticks Pass which affords the easiest passage for walkers from Thirlspot to Glenridding and Ullswater; it also provides an alternative route from the summit of the pass (2420) southward to the top of Helvellyn, or northward to Great Dodd.

From the western side of Thirlmere there are two well-known fell tracks giving access to Borrowdale; one, opposite Wythburn, climbs up the side of the gill past Harrop Tarn to Blea Tarn and so to Watendlath, the other track leaves the road farther to the north by Fisher Gill and cuts straight across the fell to Watendlath.

At Threlkeld, where the St. John's Beck joins hands with the Glanderamackin stream to swell the waters of the river Greta, you are once more back among a local community of quarrymen, farmers, and shepherds, for the Herdwick sheep which wander over the slope

[1] Sir Walter Scott's "The Bridal of Triermain."

of Saddleback belong to the valley farms. Although so strangely attached to the high pastures or "heaf" where they were reared as lambs, occasionally ewes go astray and find their way over the ridges into the wrong valleys. Twice every year, the flock-masters with their shepherds from the neighbourhood of the Skiddaw, Saddleback, and Caldbeck Fells meet at Caldbeck (the home of John Peel) and go through the business of restoring to each other the strayed sheep, not, however, without the traditional festivities common to dales-folk at these long-established and interesting meets.

THE THREE REACHES OF ULLSWATER

IV

THE LAKES AND DALES (EASTERN AREA)

I. PATTERDALE AND ULLSWATER

WORDSWORTH described Ullswater as being, " perhaps, upon the whole, the happiest combination of beauty and grandeur which any of the Lakes affords." Certainly it conforms, in its long fiord-like shape and setting amidst the high fells, to the characteristic Cumbrian type. Its head lies securely under the shelter of the wooded slopes of Glencoyne and Glenridding which, in their turn, have as a background the grand eastern flank of the Helvellyn Range, while Place Fell—its sides rising steeply to over 2000 feet—faces Glenridding across the head of the lake.

If the valley of the Eamont is approached from Penrith, which is the rail-head for Ullswater and one of the " gateways " to the Lake District, there is unfolded to the traveller, as he passes from the limestone country to the volcanic rocks, a scene of increasing interest—river, lake, and fell—until finally Patterdale is entered, where the humanized landscape of the lake shores changes to one of wild and primitive character at the dale-head. The really grand effects experienced in travelling southward are missed in the descent to Patterdale from the top of Kirkstone. The Eamont itself should not be passed quickly for it has great charm, and you may idle away the hours by its banks and watch the heron and kingfisher and possibly the elusive otter competing for its trout. Two characteristic stone bridges span the stream and connect Cumberland and Westmorland. Near Penrith is Eamont Bridge, a delightful arched structure of the fifteenth century with sturdy cutwaters still capable of supporting modern traffic, and another ancient one, Pooley Bridge, at the foot of the lake. There is the nucleus of a village at Pooley Bridge, an unpretentious row of houses and a hotel, disfigured by the proximity of untidy wooden bungalows unworthy of their position.

Looking up the lake from the steamer pier the conspicuous shape of Hallin Fell makes a fine terminal feature to the lower half of the lake, which, owing to its elbow bend, appears to end in Howtown Bay; and it is along the road to Howtown where you can obtain the finest views across the water with the impressive background of the high fells—Great Dodd, Stybarrow Dodd, and Raise—culminating in the summit of Helvellyn. Howtown consists only of the hotel and a small cluster of stone houses, but it is a good place to use as a base for the exploration of the little valleys around Martindale and the High Street Fells. Over this stretch of country roam the wild red deer, as they do also on the opposite side of the lake on Gowbarrow Fell; these are the only remaining herds still surviving in their natural state in the North of England. While on the subject of wild life it is of interest to note that in the account of a hunt (and shoot) in 1759 in the fells and woodlands of Gowbarrow, "the bag included fifteen foxes, seven badgers, eighteen wild cats, and nine martens, as well as eagles, ravens, and other species of wild life, now rare or extinct in the district." Names such as Boardale and Grisedale indicate also that in previous centuries the wild boar was common in many parts of the Lake District.

From Howtown there is a jolly track for walkers to Patterdale which leads south of Hallin Fell, across the foot of Boardale, and then skirts the fringe of the lake as a green terrace path to join the main road in Patterdale. From it is obtained a lovely prospect of the Glencoyne woodlands and Gowbarrow Park. To make a closer inspection of Gowbarrow (National Trust [1]) you must cross the lake from Howtown or follow the main road from Pooley Bridge on the western shore, which is one of the most attractive highways in Cumberland, where it follows the lake-side from Gowbarrow to Glenridding. De Quincey described Gowbarrow as " that most romantic of parks." If you enter it near the boat-landing at Aira Green you may follow the Aira Beck to the waterfall in its wooded glen. Perhaps the charm of Gowbarrow Park is explained by its lovely combination of typical wild fell, ancient forest and park trees, and views over the lake. Even Gilpin, who was not always enamoured of the scenery of the mountains, wrote that " amongst all visions of this enchanting country we had seen nothing so beautifully sublime, so elegantly picturesque, as this." [2] We will leave the reader to assess the value

[1] The three properties of the Trust on Ullswater comprise 935 acres.

[2] *Observations Relative to Picturesque Beauty.*

of his superlatives. The eighteenth-century house in its gracious setting of parkland was built by the Earl of Surrey, but the property had for generations been owned by the Howards of Greystoke, and tradition has it that Gowbarrow Park was a forest in the time of William Rufus.

About three-quarters of a mile from the Ullswater Hotel stands Stybarrow Crag. It is a beautiful rocky outcrop which overhangs the Penrith road on the western shore, and from beneath the noble beech trees you may enjoy the views across the lake to the commanding heights of Place Fell. If you follow the track up the Glencoyne Valley towards Sticks Pass, or explore—in silence—the woods and crags behind Stybarrow, you may be rewarded by the sight of buzzard and peregrine falcon and hear the croak of the raven perched on his rocky look-out. With the aid of glasses you may perhaps be lucky enough to spot the wild red deer or fallow deer as they move on the fell-side perfectly camouflaged by the russet and green of the bracken and scrub. The Glencoyne Beck marks the boundary between Westmorland and Cumberland; along its banks are good camping sites and a group of old cottages, hidden in the recesses of the glen, which possess the romantic name of Seldom Seen.

After the sylvan beauty of Glencoyne and Stybarrow it is an irritating experience to see such a banal and nondescript group of buildings in the village of Patterdale, particularly as they are situated amidst a grand and heroic landscape of mountains. The Patterdale Hotel is a building which could take its place harmoniously in any Lakeland valley of the more cultivated type, just as the "Old Swan" at Grasmere succeeds in having the appropriate character, but the Patterdale Hotel is unfortunately in proximity to an untidy and ill-designed assembly of tea-gardens, petrol filling stations and all the manifestations of the motor-tourist industry. Fortunately these disfigurements on the highway do not destroy the wild beauty of the little dales which pay tribute to Brotherswater. This—one of the smallest of the lakes—is a pleasant interlude on the journey over Kirkstone Pass. It gathers the waters of the Hartsop valley and lies amidst the small green enclosures which form the cultivated part of the dale-head. Looking southward from the road on the lake shore the visitor may enjoy the grand scenery at the valley head. Middle Dodd, between Scandale and Kirkstone Passes, stands up an acute pyramid, and behind it the beck falls like a glistening steel ribbon down the side of Caiston Glen. Screes tumble in untidy heaps down the steep slopes and appear about to overwhelm the very highway. To the west the crags stand out a dark green against the stony ridge-line of Saint Sunday Crag, and to the north the Pikes near Angle Tarn form bold silhouettes in a world of rocks, stone walls, stunted oak trees, and the never-ceasing sound of running water. Brotherswater itself, slate-grey and silent, lies at the foot of a typical lakeland valley, extending behind it to the base of Dove Crag. Near the lake the lovely cream-coloured farmhouse, Hartsop Hall, stands peacefully as if there were no other world beyond these flat green meadows, overshadowed by the craggy outline of the Fairfield group of hills. The slopes of Dove

Crag are characterized by a curious and beautiful green velvety sheen, which, with its bold outline and precipitous rocky summit, features shared with its neighbour Hart Crag, make it a superb climax to the valley head. From Brotherswater southward there is a steady and stiff climb to the summit of Kirkstone between steep fell pastures and the more precipitous slopes of Red Screes.

We have not yet mentioned another approach to Ullswater of great beauty—*via* the Cumberland Troutbeck Valley and over the Matterdale Fells to Dockray, so reaching the lake near Aira Force. The outstanding landscape features of this route are Great Mell and Little Mell Fells—two finely shaped conical hills of carboniferous limestone which are so conspicuous to the traveller from Penrith to Keswick, for they are quite detached from the main Helvellyn Range and thus dominate the lower fell country about Dacre and Penruddock.

2. MARDALE AND HAWESWATER

Before the advent of the Manchester Corporation Mardale was a pastoral paradise graced by its lovely lake and happily farmed by generations of dalesmen, each sheltering in a picturesque stone farmhouse standing in the midst of the typical lakeland holding, part valley, part fell. To-day a huge dam is being constructed across the northern end of the valley, and soon the waters will rise to those uncanny marks on the sides of the hills. The church has been demolished and the tower blown up. The friendly " Dun Bull " is to drown and a new stone-built hotel will take its place on the new road high above the level of what once was Mardale village. Strange that the thirst of Manchester should destroy the life of Mardale as earlier in the century it destroyed the beauty of Thirlmere. How often, even in our own lifetime, have our modern needs destroyed something of our country's loveliness. Railways, industry, pylons, telegraph posts, petrol stations, aerodromes, motor cars, aeroplanes, and a hundred other structures whether moving or stationary have, as it were, become nails in the coffin of destruction. Is it foolish to think this? Will our landscape absorb them as it absorbed bridges, mills, and the enclosure hedgerows and walls? We doubt it. Modern structures, at times individually pleasing, are too big in scale to fit in with our gentle landscape and too muddled in their arrangement to have a grandeur of their own. The trip north from Warrington to Carnforth should prove this. Haweswater, alas, will lose the old charm experienced so happily by all who have approached Mardale along the winding road, or dropped upon the Dun Bull from the higher land of Swindale Common or the Gate Scarth Pass.

To-day, 1937, a visit to Mardale is a strange, haunting experience. At the northern end of the valley, just beyond the lake, the great artificial dam is rising, which will bring the level of Haweswater above some of the neighbouring dwellings. South of it the farmhouses stand abandoned, empty ghosts, where happy families once enjoyed a hard, free life. It is like travelling in a country stricken with the plague, like

England during the Black Death, to follow the old road which runs so beautifully almost at water-level. One feels inclined to shout at the trees and tell them to tear up their roots and escape beyond the evil marks on the fell-sides which denote the future water-level.

Scenically Haweswater must be placed among the wilder lakes. It has much of the charm of Ennerdale, with its fine bold hillsides falling direct to the water's edge. Like Ennerdale, too, it ends in a level grassy valley which runs into the heart of the hills. Mardale and Riggindale form between them a splendid climax to the scene. A pleasant track leads to the foot of Harter Fell where it divides to follow the Nan Bield Pass to Kentmere or the Gate Scarth Pass to Long Sleddale. The hills are steep and boldly sculptured. To the right the rugged top of High Street frowns down on Riggindale and, with Kidsty Pike and Whelter Crags, almost closes the northern view. It is a solemn world at any time, and seen on a wild September evening after the mournful trip up an abandoned valley, it seemed, with a lurid orange sky, deep threatening clouds, and steep violet-coloured fells, a fit resting-place for Macbeth's witches. Even a drink at the doomed "Dun Bull" only served to heighten the melancholy. Above it, on the new road, the authorities have built a brand new stone hotel. May it prove successful, and may the scene from its windows across the reservoir to Kidsty Pike help future wanderers to forget pastoral Haweswater and to enjoy Corporation Haweswater!

BLEA TARN, LANGDALE PIKES, AND SIDE PIKE

3. LANGDALE AND ELTERWATER

Langdale provides, as it always has in the past, the main link in communications between the western dales and the more sophisticated communities at Ambleside and Windermere. Indeed those who live on the high ground above Windermere have always regarded Langdale as coming legitimately within their zone of activity whether for business or pleasure. Yet Langdale—as the reader will discover to his delight—is really a different world, in spite of the fact that the twin Pikes focus our attention in most views from Windermere and the neighbouring heights. Like symbolic beacons they call the more enterprising traveller from the luxury of hotels and railways to a simpler and harder life among the mountains, and stand as sentinels to bar the progress of all wheeled vehicles to the high fells—a land of freedom where so many rivers are born. Langdale hides its secrets from the great world of " through traffic " roads. Even though its single road has been widened, improved, and in places straightened, there is still a succession of bends which, as you pass up the winding valley, open up some fresh revelation of beauty all the way from Skelwith Bridge to the head of Mickleden. Moreover, one feels here that man has made a truce with untamed Nature, for the little green enclosures, the meadows, and valley farms, seem to express that happy state of life when the dalesman has secured control of his environment without the responsibility of riches. Not that the farms of Langdale could ever be regarded as profitable, for there is many a bad summer when the grass lies cut and rots on the wet meadows ; yet we do not see here those signs of a decayed or threatened sheep-farming industry so visible in Ennerdale and Dunnerdale and Thirlmere, nor any indication of an incessant struggle with the elements as at Wasdale Head. Langdale offers you a smiling face in spite of its wet and often snow-bound winter months.

If you enter the Rotha Valley at Clappersgate, on your way to Skelwith Bridge, there is no need to follow the main road, as an alternative and attractive by-road on the south bank of the river climbs upwards to the hamlet of Skelwith Fold and Spy Hill—rightly named, for from here there is an enchanting view into Great Langdale. Take the little footpath from the comfortable inn at Skelwith Bridge through the timber-yard to Skelwith Force. Here is a charming cascade and pool when the Brathay is in flood ; and yet more beautiful in May is the path through the carpets of bluebells in the coppice to the lovely fringe of Elter-water. There are two reaches of this little lake which can be followed through the meadows to Elterwater village, and its reedy margins are alive with mallard, coot, and water-hen, dodging here and there among the tall sedges and sending out their staccato notes of warn-ing at the approach of a stranger too near their nesting haunts. At Elterwater village the valley narrows, which entails following the road through Chapel Stile (the village of Langdale) as far as the junction of the old and new roads. Always before you are the Pikes —Pike O'Stickle and Harrison Stickle—as you follow the disused and gated road towards Dungeon Ghyll.

Here, to the old and new hotels, used to come

climbers after a twelve-mile tramp from Windermere station to try their skill on the rocks of Pavey Ark, Gimmer, and other crags of the Pikes. Now a motor service runs up the valley, and although the Langdale hotels still attract walkers and climbers from the surrounding fells, they cater also for the day tourist, and the climber passes on more frequently over Esk Hause to Wasdale. Nevertheless, Langdale, in the quiet of the early morning and evening, is one of the loveliest corners of the Lake District. There is something grand about that long level stretch of smooth turf in Mickleden, with the unchanging fell-sides sweeping down to the valley floor from Bow Fell and the Pikes. It is indeed Bow Fell which stirs the imagination in all the views in the upper half of Langdale by reason of its towering shape and cornice of precipitous crags. Except for the crude sheep-folds and " intake " walls, the primæval character of the dale-head remains unaltered by man ; yet we can give full credit to those early dalesmen who laboured to construct the graded zigzag pony-tracks which climb up the fell-side at Rosset Gill and the Stake, so affording passage for pack-horses to Wasdale and Borrowdale. Ponies, even if any could be found locally, are now very rarely met going over the Stake Pass, for the going is rough, and winter torrents have done their worst to many of the mountain tracks so that they are no longer useable by fell ponies.[1]

[1] We have occasionally met ill-advised strangers carrying bicycles over the Stake (1576 feet) to Langstrath ! They were townsmen. Similar misguided persons have also passed over Sty Head in the same manner.

The head of Langdale has two arms, separated by "The Band"—a long tongue of fell which runs in an easterly direction from Bow Fell and separates Mickleden and Oxendale which are the two arms of the valley floor. The Oxendale stream gathers its tributary becks from Crinkle Crags—the long serrated volcanic ridge which is so conspicuous on the skyline when seen from the heights above Windermere, and just where Oxendale joins the main valley is Stool End Farm, with Wall End Farm nearby on the opposite side of the beck. These two sheep farms, which include most of the enclosed pastures at the head of Langdale and have their Herdwick flocks on the surrounding fells, will fortunately not be broken up, for, owing to the generosity of Professor G. M. Trevelyan, they are now in the possession of the National Trust. The Old Dungeon Ghyll Hotel and its farm enclosures were also handed over to the Trust by the same donor. Thus permanent protection is now ensured to the foreground of the dale-head, where the little green enclosures serve as a foil to the noble background of fells—Pike O'Blisco, Crinkle Crags, Bow Fell, and Pike O'Stickle.

Lingmoor Fell separates Great Langdale from Little Langdale, and although the latter provides the route, used by the Romans, for communications between the head of Windermere and Dunnerdale, it has not been adapted for modern traffic. A narrow road winds along the valley and seems to come to a full stop in the little farmyard at Fell Foot, a typical old Westmorland farmhouse. Actually the road, unfenced, continues over Wrynose Pass but is unsuitable for motors beyond the farm. Little Langdale is charmingly enclosed by the surrounding fells. Pike O'Blisco raises his conical shape above the head of the dale, while Wetherlam and the fells of Tilberthwaite serve as the background to the small green enclosures by the river Brathay which feeds Little Langdale Tarn, drops to the main valley floor at Colwith Force, and finally enters Elter Water.

From Old Dungeon Gyhll Hotel in Great Langdale a fascinating winding road leads by Wall End Farm and Blea Tarn on the western side of Lingmoor Fell, so affording a connection with Little Langdale, the Wrynose Pass, and the high fells above Coniston.

4. GRASMERE AND THE RYDAL VALLEY

Few people who visit the Lake District fail to see both Rydal Water and Grasmere, as they lie by the side of the main traffic route from Windermere to Keswick, where a beautiful road, having passed the green meadowland by Fox How, runs in a sweeping curve below the bold rocky bluff of Nab Scar and turns sharply to the north in a cutting blasted out of the living rock.

Both are quiet stretches of water, and Rydal has tiny wooded islands and reedy shores, where the quarrelsome moorhen darts in and out of the little stony-bottomed bays, and the wagtail balances on his favourite boulder like a mechanically sprung toy. Everywhere there is a sense of poetry in the landscape, and it is little wonder that Wordsworth found a happy retreat amidst the romantic scenery of these russet fells. Indeed he has helped to give Grasmere and

7

Rydal Water a wider fame even than their own loveliness could have achieved unaided. His footsteps have lingered by many a gateway as he watched some passing effect of the clouds or caught a glimpse of some tiny group of wild flowers. His personality seems to pervade the scene, and in some way he seems to have created the lakes, rivers, and mountains through the magic of his verses.

The long slopes of the Fairfield range rise immediately to the north and east, beginning that vast mountain mass which culminates in Helvellyn. To the south and west are Loughrigg, most familiar of fells, and Silver How, an outlier of the Langdale group. Beneath their slopes, on the southern shore of Rydal Water, runs an enchanting terrace track which leads to the river Rotha and to the pretty woods which cover the spit of flat land separating Rydal and Grasmere. Here, in early summer, bluebells carpet the ground and help to create, with the murmuring stream, the little wooden foot-bridge, and the fresh green foliage, one of those inimitable lakeland pictures which combine the soft tranquillity of the sheltered valley with the vigorous background of rocky fells.

A steep road leads from Skelwith Bridge past Loughrigg Tarn, and continues down Red Bank to the western shores of Grasmere. There the sleepy village nestles under the shadow of the fells, and for eight months of the year has little but the bleating of sheep and the lowing of cattle to disturb its rural seclusion. For the remaining four months it shakes off its winter lethargy and offers hospitality to crowds of visitors. From Grasmere there are entrancing walks, short or strenuous, towards all the points of the compass, for it lies snugly under the lee of its hills in the very centre of the great Lakeland area. For example, the visitor may explore the wild scenery of Helvellyn where the wind howls over the shoulder of Striding Edge, or climb over the fell to Grisedale and the unsurpassed scenery at the head of Ullswater. Again, he can visit Easedale Tarn or follow the track which leads up Far Easedale, pass over Greenup and drop down to Stonethwaite and the wooded splendour of Borrowdale, and he is never far from the beauty of Langdale or the high solitude of Scandale.

Grasmere is famous also for the Sports, and many visitors during this annual event gain their first impression of a typically Lakeland scene. It is an unusual experience for a stranger to watch several pairs of wrestlers in the ring at the same time, crouching in the Cumberland and Westmorland style with interlocked arms waiting for the exact moment to tighten a grip and throw an opponent, and exciting, too, to witness the "guides" race up and down the side of the steep fell behind the thronged arena, or watch through glasses the competing foxhounds as they follow the trail into the surrounding landscape. Could there be a more perfect setting? Let your eyes leave the crowd in the arena and wander over the whole range of hills which surround the colourful pageant of summer—Nab Scar, Stone Arthur, and the magnificent forms of Seat Sandal : Helm Crag which guards the approach to Dunmail Raise, the legendary site of the death of a king long since forgotten : Easedale disappearing into the distant hills, and Silver How rising proudly above the still waters of the lake. All these constitute a grand background to the cluster of stone dwellings and little shops watched over by the solid square church tower on the river's bank. The fertile green meadows, the swiftly running stream, and a still, smooth stretch of water, reflecting like a mirror the highly coloured hills which surround it, all contribute to the picture. The crowd will cease to exist for you then and there will remain only the friendly beauty of the hills with their never-failing message of welcome, like a perfect hostess, putting you at your ease without affectation.

If the visitor is fortunate he may see later in the year another local scene : fox-hunting carried out on foot. From Nab Cottage on the banks of Rydal Water he might watch the hounds, little white specks, climbing up the steep side of Loughrigg Fell, their cry filling the whole of the valley and echoing among the mountains. Groups of figures stand silhouetted on the ridge, or move singly or in groups from one vantage-point to the next. There are few who can keep pace with a local pack of foxhounds to the finish of a hunt, yet there is no more exhilarating experience on one of these late autumn days, when the hills are sharply defined against a clear blue sky and the air is filled with the magic fragrance of bracken and heather. It is possible, then, to forget one is a visitor, a mere looker-on, and to become part of the life of this grand country ; to fade with the hounds and the huntsman into the scene. On these occasions the local dialect may be heard in its purest form as dalesman or shepherd on the fellside shouts directions to the huntsman if they have " viewed " the fox. The dialect and traditions of Westmorland and Cumberland are derived from Norse rather than Saxon as so many place-names and local expressions indicate, and this perhaps helps to account for that curious effect of the Lakeland landscape which, in its most sublime moods, seems to call one to the pagan worship of some mountain god with no deeper doctrine than light and shade, colour, and the beauty of Nature's forms.

On two other occasions there is the opportunity to witness the vitality of local life in the valley, at the annual " Rush-bearing," and on the production of the Grasmere Play. The latter is specially written and produced by local residents, and members of the cast are selected from people whose normal occupations are in the neighbourhood. Quite apart from the dramatic value of the Grasmere plays, they help to record the customs and vigorous dialect of Westmorland folk, and to stimulate local patriotism.

From Rydal a very beautiful quiet road follows down the west bank of the river Rotha, winding along the foot of the Loughrigg slopes ; it passes the well-worn " stepping-stones " and under magnificent trees, finally meeting the Langdale and Waterhead roads at Rotha Bridge. This route avoids the traffic of the main road and serves as a more fitting link between the virginal beauty of Rydal Water and the cultivated scenery of Windermere.

5. WINDERMERE AND ESTHWAITE

Any attempt to portray the character of Windermere's landscape must take account of the seasons,

for this—the largest and most popularly known of our English lakes—presents the greatest contrast of scene between winter and summer.

There are some days in mid-winter when it has a rare beauty, not only on those infrequent brilliant days when the shimmering lake is seen against a background of snow-capped mountains and blue sky, but more often when the sombre landscape is suddenly enlivened by broad shafts of pale sunlight which pierce the grey clouds, transforming the leaden surface of the lake into polished steel and throwing into coloured relief the red bracken and glistening rocks of the fell-sides. As seen from any promontory on the lake shore on such a day, nothing disturbs the serenity of the great expanse of water, except perhaps little flotillas of mallard, teal, coot, and moorhen, as they forage for their winter feed in and out of the reedy bays or hurry across the lake to some island refuge. During the long winter months, when the water-fronts and hotels at Bowness and Ambleside stand forlorn and deserted by their summer crowds, the lake becomes the home of a great many species of native wild-fowl and rarer migrants which have abandoned normal haunts on the frozen upland tarns. Some indeed come far from the tidal estuaries on the fringe of the Lake District, and in early spring and late autumn it is no uncommon sight to see or hear the flocks of grey-lag geese as they pass like a spear-head over the lake to and fro between the Solway Firth and their feeding grounds farther south. For the winter walker, the lower fell country about Windermere offers an infinite variety of delights, when distant views of

THE HEAD OF WINDERMERE FROM JENKINS CRAG

blue mountains are enhanced as they appear in silhouette above valley mists. There are innumerable little lanes leading northward by Orrest Head to Applethwaite Common and Troutbeck, or southward in the direction of Winster, Ghyll Head Tarn, and Cartmel Fell, which here and there reveal entrancing views of the lake and the high western fells beyond. Even a winter's drive along the main road from Ambleside to Newby Bridge offers unexpected glimpses of lake and mountains not possible when the trees are covered with their thick summer foliage.

But springtime and autumn are Nature's pageants in the Lake District. In April, May and early June the journey from the smoke-begrimed towns of Lancashire to Newby Bridge and Windermere is a revelation, for the mixed woodlands of chestnut, birch, beech, and oak, combined here and there with the bright green shoots of the young larch, create an intoxicating medley of colour. It is in springtime also that the warm southern valleys of the Lake District can show orchards gay with a mass of plum blossom, and the coppice woods are adorned with a carpet of primroses, daffodils and wild hyacinths.

For those who approach Windermere by road from the south there is a choice of three routes with little traffic which enfold to the traveller much of the beauty of the lower fells so characteristic of the Silurian rocks, and the gentle valleys which run southward to Morecambe Bay. The first is from Kendal to Bowness *via* Crook, affording a succession of fine views down the valleys, and finally, from the top of Cleabarrow Hill, suddenly appears the prospect of the lake and the distant Coniston Fells. The second—from Kendal to Newby Bridge—crosses the river Winster at Bowland Bridge, and then climbs steeply over Cartmel Fell where, close to Gummers How, there is revealed another attractive bird's-eye view of Lakeside and the Leven valley. The third route skirts the southern lowland country from Levens *via* Lindale to Newby Bridge and its pleasant inn by the riverside. There is always a fascinating charm and quietude about this gentle river that nothing seems to destroy and which entices one to spend hours or days idling by its reedy margins, or paddling along its winding course out into the smooth expanse of the lake. The swans nest in its little back-waters, the otter chases its trout, while the kingfisher adds a flash of iridescent colour, and the screaming swifts dart under the ancient stone arches of the bridge and make joyous spirals over the musical waters of the weir.

Summer brings with it to Windermere the happy crowds of tourists and trippers, by steamer, train, by car and motor coach. More than any other lake it is pleasure-ridden during the short holiday season. Yet in spite of this, and at any time of the year, nothing could deprive Windermere of the essential elements of its natural beauty. For example, there are its lovely islands, large and small, which add so much diversity of interest to the lake with their fine trees, little glades, and rocky outcrops ; the steep wooded slopes of Claife Heights protecting the western shore and facing the green meadows of Calgarth and the Vale of Troutbeck across the water ; above all, the superb climax at the head of the lake where Fairfield and its supporting high fells rise majestically beyond the roofs of Ambleside. These, indeed, are only a few of the unchanging features which have withstood the passage of time and man's attempt at "improvement."

It might be said that Windermere has none of those dramatic qualities possessed by some of the other lakes where the close proximity of high rocky mountains provides a setting of wildness and grandeur ; indeed, Bowness Bay and Belle Isle suggest to some merely the skilful work of the landscape artist. Yet no artifice of man could have produced the subtle transition between the lower and upper reaches of the lake which is effected by the "narrows" near Cockshott Point, by the islands, and the slightly crescent shape of the lake itself. The serene and cultivated beauty of Windermere is of a different order, and to appreciate this fully the visitor should travel by boat from Lakeside to Water Head, and he will then experience a gradual crescendo of landscape interest throughout its ten miles of navigable water.

The scenery of the southern reach of the lake below Rawlinson Nab has all the quiet charm of a wide river, with its wooded shores, occasional meadows and little boathouses ; only from Fell Foot is there a glimpse of the higher fells by Coniston, as all western views are shut off by the hills behind Graythwaite. Storrs Hall Hotel—once a Regency mansion with a tragic history of past owners—is as finely situated for landscape effect as one could wish, facing south down the lake on a promontory ; but it has long since lost its park-lands, which are now developed for little villas with their trim gardens, and larger country houses on the rising slopes behind. Here and there the builders have made an unfortunate choice of red roofs, but the magnificent trees and gardens compensate for this sophisticated and urbanized fringe of the lake shores. Only two islands, Blake Holme and Rampholme, interrupt the long southern reach, but on the western shore a characteristic rocky island, Ling Holme, marks the exit of the Cunsey Beck and Esthwaite Valley, where little stone or white-washed farmhouses still form part of the pastoral scene as it existed in Wordsworth's time. A different scene greets the summer visitor north of the old coach ferry. Belle Isle with its magnificent park-like trees and green lawns, its circular eighteenth-century mansion and little farm buildings, has succeeded admirably in maintaining its dignity and charm as a private domain, yet it is just opposite all the bustle and democratic gaiety of Bowness Bay, with its jolly assembly of launches, yachts, and every type of small craft, its steamer piers, hotels, and boat-houses.

Nothing is more harmonious in the summer scene on Windermere than the shapely hulls of small racing yachts as they tack to and fro on the upper reach, their snow-white sails and gay pennons contrasting against a background of trees. Long may these survivals of a non-mechanical and more leisured age continue to hold their own against the recent innovation of speed-boats, whose noisy engines have done so much to disturb the beauty of the lake and rob it of its former peace for both residents and visitors. Yet even at holiday-time you can easily avoid the crowds at Bowness and Water Head by rowing to the more secluded bays and islands, or by crossing to the western shore and then wandering along the shady lakeside road and lanes to High Wray and the solitude of Blelham Tarn ; or you can penetrate up the little streams and through the reeds and inlets of Pull Wyke and Lily Bay, where only the song of the warbler or the plaintive cry of a sandpiper will break the silence. The northern half of Windermere, under favourable conditions, is incomparable, when sunlight and cloud shadows make a moving coloured pattern across its wide expanse of water and on the brown slopes of Loughrigg and Wansfell. There are more intimate pictures of river scenery also for those who care to paddle up the swiftly running streams at the head of the lake, where the Brathay and Rotha, charged with the rains from the heart of the high fells, wind their sinuous course through meadows to the lake.

Scarcely two miles from Windermere as the crow flies, Esthwaite lies securely hidden between the protecting heights of Claife and the woodlands of Grizedale. In winter or summer Esthwaite Lake, watched over by the ancient church at Hawkshead, seems to be at peace with the world, and there is nothing to disturb the quiet beauty of its waters. At Grizedale the native woodlands will be invaded by the plantations of the Forestry Commission, but the open meadows by the shores of Esthwaite will now be secure for all time. There is, too, the glory of the beeches of Rusland. This lovely valley, remote from traffic and noise, and one of the most precious fragments of native woodland scenery in the district, is typical of the lowland country in Furness yet easily accessible from Newby Bridge or Hawkshead.

6. CONISTON

The most beautiful road approach to Coniston Water is from Ambleside, either by crossing Brathay Bridge and so to the high-level road which passes the Barngate Inn, or by the main road across Skelwith Bridge and over Oxenfell. The former route enjoys a grand long-range view over Windermere to the high fells around High Street, and approaches the head of Coniston Lake down a steep corkscrew bend; the latter takes the traveller through the enchanting scenery of Yewdale to Coniston village.

The walker from Brathay Bridge would be rewarded if he followed the little road above the river up to Skelwith Fold—a cluster of cottages and a typical old Lakeland farmhouse with local character and great charm; thence by lane and footpath to Tarn Hows. Here he could see the effect of informal plantations of fir trees which give a certain picturesque quality to one of the best-known tarns of the lower fells. This is perhaps the most attractive and favourite picnic place near Coniston, and full of colour when the heather and dark firs are reflected in the placid waters of the tarn; it might indeed be taken as an example to justify the judicious planting of conifers in the Lake District; but it is a very different thing from the regimented formality of the great plantations of spruce which have so sadly damaged the beauty of the fell-sides on Whinlatter Pass. From Tarn Hows a short shady path leads down Glen Mary by the beck-side into Yewdale.

The village of Coniston stands a little way from the lake, the older part clustered along the sides of the ravine cut by Church Beck, which at times comes down as a raging torrent, for it gathers all the storm water from the high mountain tarns and becks of Brim Fell and Wetherlam. Church Beck is, indeed, the centre of life and justification for the existence of Coniston as a village community, because high up its course on the fell-sides are the old copper workings with their inevitable untidy debris; and generations of local folk have passed up and down the beck-sides between the mine and their rather grim cottage homes. And if the visitor cares to join the groups leaning over the bridge where the road crosses the beck he will hear farm-hands and shepherds and quarrymen from Tilberthwaite exchanging gossip in their local dialect on current affairs.

Hotels, boarding-houses, Victorian villas, and a few larger houses, together with a railway station perched strangely high above the cottage roofs, go to make up the picture of a village which cannot lay claim to architectural distinction; yet it has a grand background of high fells and in front the long river-like lake running southward to the woodlands by Nibthwaite. A very beautiful lake-side road runs along the eastern shore at the foot of the wooded fell-side; it leads to Nibthwaite, passes close to the only two islands of the lake, and throughout its length affords really fine views of the "Old Man," Dow Crag, and the whole group of Coniston Fells. Unlike the western shores of the lake by Torver, the eastern side offers in June a sight of surpassing colour and beauty. Although in many counties bluebells carpet the woodlands in spring, never have we seen as here a whole hillside crimson with foxgloves. Devon and Somerset have their walls adorned with foxgloves, making coloured lines on the landscape, but here on the eastern shores of Coniston Lake there are acres which Nature paints crimson at midsummer. In late autumn, too, the woodlands at the head of the lake, and especially in Yewdale, are resplendent with gorgeous red and orange tints, while the ravine and cascades of Tilberthwaite are still lined with the refreshing green of innumerable ferns and lichens. Little wonder that John Ruskin, with such an environment, should have been content to make Coniston his home for so many years, where he described lovingly and with much understanding the natural beauty of the Lakeland scene.

V

THE FRINGE OF THE LAKE DISTRICT

AT Three Shires Stone on the top of Wrynose Pass, the three counties of Cumberland, Westmorland, and Lancashire join hands. Cumberland possesses, in fact, the lion's share of the grandest and highest western fells, for its boundary follows the river Duddon from the sea to Wrynose, thence along the watersheds to the middle of the Helvellyn Range and so down the centre of Ullswater and the River Eamont to the Eden valley. Thus roughly the western half of the Lake District proper (*i.e.* the potential National Park area) comes within the administrative county of Cumberland. Westmorland possesses the second largest portion—the eastern part of the district, while Lancashire claims the small salient of Furness which lies between the Duddon Valley and the Winster valley, but excluding Windermere Lake.

Hence, all three counties are intimately concerned in the administration and future preservation of the Lake District which, for all purposes, should be regarded as a single geographical unit. On the "Fringe" of the region, however, the character of the landscape differs considerably in the three counties. In Cumberland there is the level coastal plain, and on the north the northern plain extending to Carlisle. The

Westmorland fringe is a combination of bleak uplands and well-wooded valleys, of high moorland scenery with wide prospects across the Vale of Eden towards the Pennine escarpment. The Lancashire fringe consists of long bracken covered or wooded ridges rising above wide sandy estuaries only covered by the infrequent high tides. There is a feeling of sheltered warmth in these cultivated southern valleys in striking contrast to the long exposed coastline of Cumberland and the wilder windswept heights of Shap Fells.

1. CUMBERLAND

Carlisle, the county town, is outside the subject of this book, but it cannot be entirely ignored, as it commands all the northern approaches to the Lake District and the Solway coast ; it possesses a distinctive character as an historic border city, with a cathedral of much interest, and it lies in close proximity to the splendid uplands of Northumberland which proudly carry the Roman Wall across Britain from the Solway to Newcastle. The traveller from Carlisle may follow either of two excellent roads—the western one to Cockermouth and the coastal ports or the eastern one to Penrith, for both these towns are gateways to the Lake District. From the Penrith road he may diverge to explore the valley of the Caldew and the village of Caldbeck. All the way from Carlisle to Cockermouth or Penrith one passes through a somewhat curious landscape, in places consisting of rough or cultivated uplands reminiscent of some of the Middle Marches on the Border, and in other parts of green sheltered valleys divided into a variety of striped enclosures by hedges and stone walls. But all the way the countryside is enlivened by the same characteristics of Cumbrian and Border architecture—little grey stone buildings with coloured surrounds to doors and windows, giving welcome contrast to the general low tones of roofs and walls. In certain places, also, red sandstone gives added notes of colour to the scene. Always before you on the journey south there is the distant outline of the Lakeland fells, and particularly the fine group of high moorlands leading up to Skiddaw—a land of soft rounded hills providing the rough pastures for black-faced sheep and cheviots from the Caldbeck farms.

Caldbeck itself is a typical Cumbrian village on the northern edge of the Skiddaw Range, built of stone and famous for its association with John Peel; its ancient church stands on the river's bank and the sound of the rushing waters fills the whole building. The landscape of these northern fells and moors, which can be explored from Caldbeck, is very different from the high volcanic fells and dramatic scenery of the western dales; only in the southern and eastern sides of Saddleback do the slate hills show their precipitous crags and ridges.

The road from Caldbeck through Hesket Newmarket and Mungrisdale skirts the eastern flanks of the northern fells, crossing all the little streams which pay tribute to the Caldew. The Caldew itself drains the heart of the great expanse of moorland in Skiddaw Forest, and its upper reaches can be followed from the hamlet of Mosedale by the farm track to Swineside, where a fine flock of sheep roam the hills or fatten on the riverside enclosures. Beyond Swineside the track continues to an old lead mine under Carrock Fell, and beyond, to the single lonely house amidst the heather and headwaters of the Caldew between Skiddaw and Saddleback. The valley to the west of Mungrisdale village is more dramatic. Here it is almost closed by the steep side of Bowscale Fell and Bannerdale Crags, whose precipitous slopes afford a grand background to the valley scenery.

From Mungrisdale to Penrith the country opens out into green meadows and enclosed pastures dominated by two isolated limestone hills, Great Mell Fell and Little Mell Fell. Here, too, is the gracious park of Greystoke Castle close to its lovely village and one of the finest churches of the Lake District.

Cumberland's share of the coastal plain extends from Cockermouth to the Duddon Sands. It is a countryside of pleasant undulating farm lands, attractive sand-dunes on the coast, and the foothills of the greater lakeland fells. Few people realize how impressive the mountains can appear from the plain which serves as a foil, and magnifies the grandeur and height of the hills, especially when their summits are collecting the ominous clouds of a coming storm. Cockermouth, in spite of its proximity to the industrial areas, has all the atmosphere and quiet dignity of an old market town. Its long, wide street flanked by harmonious flat-fronted houses and shops has the proper urbane quality. The ancient castle, which seems to mount guard over the town, has a splendid site and commands a view of rare charm to the north across water-meadows and woodlands. To the south of Cockermouth is the pleasant but undistinguished countryside which at Lamplugh introduces the well-defined fringe of western fells. Here rise the steep slopes of Murton Fell and Blake Fell, like outposts of that grand company of hills which separate Ennerdale from Crummock and Loweswater. Round the western fringe of this country a high, rough fell road leads from Lamplugh to Roughton, affording magnificent views across Ennerdale Lake to the superb range of mountains which culminate in Scoat Fell and Pillar. Another characteristic road which skirts the western fells is that which runs over the open moorland from Ennerdale Bridge and across Cold Fell to Calder Bridge, where the splendid but melancholy ruins of the Abbey lie almost hidden beneath huge trees by the river. The Calder itself may be followed upstream far up into the fells—a lonely tract of country leading to the greater heights of Scoat Fell and Haycock.

The coast consists of long sandy beaches and flat grassy margins. Seascale, in spite of its undistinguished Victorian buildings, is the most conveniently situated centre on the coast from which to explore the western dales or that surprising muddy estuary where the Irt, Mite, and Esk discharge their clear mountain streams. Above this little resort on the slopes of Muncaster Fell, Muncaster Castle, in its attractive gardens, watches over the flat, green meadows where the Esk meanders towards the sea. There is a fascination for the bird-watcher in this lowland landscape ; the melodious cry of the curlew rises above the wind in the grasses, and the entertaining antics of little waders and other marsh birds enliven the scene. Ravenglass, its ancient port deprived of former activity by the silting up of the harbour, stands a little forlorn and deserted in its setting of grassy foreshore, mud banks, and sea. It is reminiscent of some of the forgotten little seaports of East Anglia.

To the south of Muncaster Fell the whole landscape is dominated by the form of Black Combe, a grand and detached outpost of the Lakeland mountains ; it rises steeply from the road itself, and if viewed from far distant places on the Fylde coast of Lancashire, it appears as a bold headland rising directly from the sea. Few of the higher Lakeland hills dominate their surroundings so completely as Black Combe, and it compels the road traveller's respect by forcing him to make a wide detour to reach any of the more southern dales or lakes. Beyond Black Combe lie the broad sands of Duddon which penetrate almost to Broughton, and the tall chimney of Millom, which at night send out their sinister lurid glare like beacons across the coast of Furness. At Duddon Bridge, where the wide sandy estuary forms such a glorious contrast to the impressive shape of Black Combe, the traveller crosses into Lancashire.

2. LANCASHIRE

The scenery in the Lancashire fringe is striking different from that in Cumberland. Whereas the latter has a narrow belt of sea coast and meadow and a dominating range of hills ending in Black Combe, Lancashire's fringe is broken by bracken-covered ridges and sandy estuaries. The hills are lower and often covered with trees ; the valleys are warmer and more cultivated ; above all there is a greater sense of population.

The road from Broughton eastward across the flat meadow-land of the Duddon Valley rises sharply above Grizebeck. From this higher open country it affords magnificent prospects of the fells above Dunnerdale and the Coniston group. At Greenodd it meets the head of the Cartmel Sands, the second of the sandy estuaries, where the flat marshes and sandy creeks extend for some miles before they meet the open sea. From Greenodd the road leads by Haverthwaite and Backbarrow, with its blue dye factory, to Newby Bridge. The two centres from which to explore this isolated section of Lancashire are Grange over Sands or Newby Bridge itself. The whole of the Cartmel peninsula is interesting—Holker Park containing one of the few large houses of the district, and the charming village of Cartmel where the Priory dominates the cluster of picturesque houses, its open bracken-covered moors, and its flat seashore. Here the long views across Morecambe Bay and the Pennine Chain and the Forest of Bowland compensate the visitor for the flatness of the foreground. The low road from Flookburgh to Haverthwaite is interesting from its contrasted landscape of marshland and fell ; and the high road from Cartmel, past High Gate Side and Bigland Hall to Backbarrow is refreshingly open with wide views to the north.

A little lane leads down to the shore from Allithwaite to Kents Bank. From this point, before the construction of good turnpike roads and railways, wagons and pack-horses used to make their hazardous crossing of the sands to Hest Bank near Lancaster. Only at low tide could this be accomplished, and there are many old records of the loss of transport in the difficult sinking sand of Warton Sands.

The county boundary follows the river Winster, so that Lancashire shares with Westmorland this green valley dominated by the limestone mass of Whitbarrow.

3. WESTMORLAND

The Westmorland portion of the Lakeland fringe is traversed by the great northern road which passes Levens Bridge and Kendal, and takes the long hill of Shap in its stride. It is a wild, bleak country of rounded hills and deeply cut valleys, where rivers run in beds covered with small boulders, and where the soft green meadowland, so characteristic of the Lake District, is largely absent. It is a country notorious in winter, when drifts of snow block the roads to traffic, and biting winds numb the fingers and chill the bones of the lorry drivers. It has a grandeur born of this very bleakness, and as the road rises from the valley near Kendal into the open country it passes between red, black, and white posts which mark the margin of the road. On the west lie the foothills which lead to High Street ; on the east the uncultivated uplands which carry the elevated landscape of the Lake District to the very border of the Pennine Chain.

North of Shap, where a noisy procession of motor

traffic passes through its long street, the road skirts Lowther Park. Here it is wise to leave the main route and follow the quiet by-road which leads to Askham village. This is perhaps the most lovely village and parkland which Westmorland possesses and a welcome contrast to the wilder moorland only a mile or two away. A bridge, two churches, and the castle itself add architectural interest to the natural background. The village of Askham which adjoins the park is indeed one of the unspoilt villages of England, with its wide green, studded with trees, its characteristic stone houses, and the view into open country at the southern end.

Appleby, the capital of Westmorland, may legitimately be brought into the fringe, for it is a town of great charm and character with its ancient castle standing grandly above the Eden, and its wide street with picturesque monuments at each end. As an administrative and market centre it has, however, long since taken second place to Kendal.

VI

THE LOCAL BUILDING TRADITION

In all mountainous or isolated districts it is usual to find that the old building traditions persist long after new materials and a new technique of design and construction have resulted elsewhere in different architectural forms. This is the case, as we would expect to find, in the Lake District, where the difficulties and the cost of transport chiefly determine the choice of materials.

In the dales, where good roads were few or non-existent, and stone available everywhere, the first settlers relied on the nearest quarry, whence stone was drawn by " sleds " or rough carts to the site selected for farmhouse and outbuildings, usually conveniently near a beck and the valley meadows, and yet having an " out-run " to the open fell pastures. So we find most of the fell farms and their cottages admirably sited for their purpose and harmonizing perfectly with their surroundings. Wherever possible stone was employed—rough stone from the boulder-strewn slopes of the fells for the dry fence walls which formed the enclosures or " intakes " from the fell: the better quarry stone laid with lime mortar for the domestic and farm buildings. Lintels, door and window jambs, round chimneys, indeed everything possible

FELL FARMS AT WHITBECK

was constructed in stone. The paving and dairy slabs were in thick slates, the roofs of grey-green small slates laid with diminishing courses, and to a fairly low pitch as this method economized in roof timbers and scaffolding. Simple hardwood joinery for doors, windows, and fittings completed the essential elements of small domestic buildings. There was little evidence of conscious attempts at design, and only the minimum of craftsmen's decoration; perhaps an entrance door here and there with carved monogram and date stone, or a solid carved oak dresser in the living-room. In some cases, also, there would be an outside spinning gallery [1] in oak with roof extension over; here was made the rough home-spun cloth with wool shorn from the farmer's Herdwick flock.

Although the stone for external walls was laid in mortar with a slight fall outwards and so waterproof, many of the early builders on exposed sites took the precaution to render the outsides of their dwellings with a thick coating of roughcast plaster, lime-whitened and sometimes coloured in delightful shades—yellow, orange, pale blue, and occasionally pink—so giving a friendly and altogether charming note of colour and contrast in the landscape. The long, low proportions, with simple gabled roof, string and drip courses to protect the walls, and generous porches, gave entirely satisfying results.

Such then were the earliest domestic buildings of the Lake District, the traditions and technique being

[1] Examples may be seen at Helm Farm, Bowness; Hodge Hall, Cartmel Fell; High Yewdale Farm, Tilberthwaite, and Lower Hartsop near Patterdale.

passed on without a break from father to son with little change except the substitution of sash windows for casements about the end of the eighteenth century.

A few more substantial houses were built and occupied by the more well-to-do classes and yeomen. Typical of this class is the house at Town End, Troutbeck, occupied by the same family since 1626 and here illustrated (see page 123), and Old Calgarth Hall, in the same valley near Windermere. It was not until the coming of the railway to Windermere and Keswick about the middle of the last century, bringing with it new residents from the towns with the latest Victorian fashions, that the domestic buildings of the region became more pretentious and, in many cases, quite unsuitable for the locality. For the most part, however, the robust character and simplicity of the earlier work was still followed in farm buildings of stone, with the door and window openings of barns and cow-sheds outlined by margins of whitewash, and with tall or squat circular pillars of rough stone forming an elementary kind of Doric Order to the open cart-sheds.[1]

In larger mansions, of which there are but few in this district, the more elaborate details of Tudor and Renaissance features may be seen ; but in these cases the finer masonry work required for doorways, windows, and cornices was executed in " freestone " or in certain parts in red sandstone hauled from more distant quarries. Levens Hall is an outstanding example of

[1] On most farms there are examples of the squat columns. Tall colonnades may be seen at Skelwith Bridge for example, now converted to form part of a dwelling.

an early manor house, set in its lovely garden where topiary work can be seen at its best.

So far we have mentioned only a few isolated examples to illustrate the traditional methods of building, but equally characteristic examples of farm and cottage groups can be seen in all the less frequented places throughout the district. It is, however, rare to find complete villages, such as survive in other counties, where there are not additions and intrusions by the late Victorian builders. The town of Windermere is itself a product of the Railway Age, and there is practically nothing remaining of the original hamlet of Birthwaite near the railway station. On the other hand, at Bowness, where modern shops and sham half-timber have damaged its native architecture, there is still a cluster of pleasant little eighteenth-century cottages hidden behind the church, itself a notable example of the local building tradition with its curious painted nave. Rydal and Grasmere have not suffered so much from modern intrusions. Keswick has spread its villas and hotels over the surrounding lands, but the centre of the town has retained a marked individuality, partly by reason of its narrow streets, but more particularly in its old market-place where the seventeenth-century colour-washed town hall presides over the centre of all activities ; this building is a happy combination of local style blended with the gaiety of the continental tradition, perhaps due to the old German settlers who worked the local mines. Broughton-in-Furness is also distinguished by the pleasant formality of its little central square entirely enclosed by buildings.

Among all the little communities of the Lake District Hawkshead is without a rival for the beauty of its site, the compact arrangement, and the harmony of its buildings, all unified by its church well placed on elevated ground overlooking Esthwaite. There are no straggling suburbs or discordant appendages to disfigure the surroundings, and this picturesque little town survives to-day without any material change and much as it must have appeared when Wordsworth visited the ancient church and grammar school. There are mediæval remains near Hawkshead Hall of archæological interest, but with this exception there are no individual buildings of special merit ; yet Hawkshead proves how the right choice of colour and materials can be entirely successful in maintaining the local character and atmosphere.

There are several villages which, though not achieving the same degree of harmony as Hawkshead, can show pleasant groups of buildings which adorn the landscape. In the west of the region, the villages of Lamplugh, Loweswater, Brackenthwaite, and Braithwaite are notable ; in Borrowdale, there is no happier composition than the little collection of buildings by the bridge at Grange, while at Rosthwaite and Seatoller there are most satisfactory groups of cottages and farms. Even more characteristic of the old dalehead village is Stonethwaite, appearing as though it had grown out of the rocks of its lovely valley.

It is fitting that we should conclude our brief survey of the Lakeland Landscape by an appeal to those who may build in this delectable corner of England. The poet Gray, after a visit to the Vale of Grasmere, wrote :

SEVENTEENTH-CENTURY HOUSE, TROUTBECK, WESTMORLAND

"Not a single red tile, no flaring gentleman's house or garden-wall, breaks in upon the repose of this little unsuspected paradise ; but all is peace, rusticity, and happy poverty, in its neatest and most becoming attire." The words of Wordsworth himself, in his admirable *Guide to the Lakes*, contain the soundest advice on the colour and form of buildings and on the planting of trees. The principles that he expounded remain valid to-day, for it is the avoidance of discordant colours in building, regard for simplicity of form, and the right choice of local materials for walls and roofs, which are the essential conditions for every new building if it is to be absorbed into this grand landscape of mountain, fell, and lake. Here Nature is dominant. Man's puny efforts must be subservient and unobtrusive.

APPENDIX

FREEHOLD AND LEASEHOLD PROPERTIES OF THE NATIONAL TRUST IN THE LAKE DISTRICT

Locality.	Name of Property.	Approx. Acreage.	Remarks.
Ambleside .	Borrans Field .	20	Near the head of Windermere, containing remains of a Roman fort (Galava) excavated and left exposed.
,, .	Bridge House .	—	On the Rydal road, a seventeenth-century small building on the crown of a bridge.
,, .	Kelsick Scar .	14	Near Jenkin Crag, on the slopes of Wansfell : woodland commanding fine prospect of Windermere.
,, .	Land, Lake Road	—	A small field with views to the west.
,, .	Wray Castle . .	64	Beautiful park and farm lands on the west shore of Windermere, with country house of nineteenth century.
,, .	Bee Holme . .	—	A small island between Wray and Pull Wyke.

Locality.	Name of Property.	Approx. Acreage.	Remarks.
Borrowdale, nr. Keswick	Castle Crag . .	18	A prominent hill close to Grange, rising abruptly to 900 feet and commanding a splendid view of Derwentwater. Reputed site of ancient British fort.
,, .	Grange Fell and the Bowder Stone	310	Typical example of fell land, extending from the river Derwent to the top of King's How (1365 ft.) and including the "Borrowdale Birches."
,, .	Peace Howe . .	—	A good view-point near Grange, commanding Derwentwater.
Buttermere .	Buttermere, Crummock, and Loweswater	1317	The three lakes, together with Burtness and Hasness Plantations, Long How, Lanthwaite, Wood, Holme Wood, Scale Force, and land by the Honister road. Additional lands are protected by covenants.
Coniston .	Land near lake .	20	Near the southern end of the lake.
,, .	Peel Island and Woodland	—	—
,, .	Land near Nibthwaite	116	Between Nibthwaite and Selside (600 ft.).

Locality.	Name of Property.	Approx. Acreage.	Remarks.
Derwentwater	Brandelhow . .	108	On the west shore of the lake. Fine woodlands under the slopes of Cat Bells and extending to the lake.
”	Manesty . .	115	Adjoining Brandelhow: woodland, park, and rough land, with part of the lake and manorial and fishing rights.
”	Crow Park, Cockshott Wood, Castle Head, and North Strands Hagg	80	Between Keswick and Derwentwater. Open space safeguarding the fringe of the lake.
”	Friar's Crag, Lord's Island, and Calf Close Bay	17	On the east side of the lake, near Keswick: memorials to John Ruskin and the late Canon Rawnsley.
”	Rampsholme .	—	A small island opposite Calf Close Bay.
”	Stables Hill and Broomhill Point	57	Farm and woodland near Keswick, adjoining Calf Close Bay, with a house and cottage.
”	South Strands Hagg	20	Affords a link between Stables Hill and Friar's Crag.
Duddon Valley	Cockley Beck and Dale Head Farms	1200	At the dale-head including Wrynose Bottom and joining up with the Monk Coniston property at the Carrs (2500 ft.).
”	Wallowbarrow Crag	84	Near Seathwaite—rough fell land.
”	Crag End Wood .	—	Adjoining the above.

Locality.	Name of Property.	Approx. Acreage.	Remarks.
Ennerdale .	Ennerdale . .	3624	Fell lands of which 3350 acres are held on a 500-year lease, and are above 1000 feet.
Fell and Rock Club Memorial, near Wasdale Head	Fell and Rock Climbing Club War Memorial	3000	Magnificent area of high fells all above the 1500-ft. contour, embracing Great Gable and many of the highest summits and best climbing country.
Grasmere .	Boothwaite . .	½	Part of the Commonfield in Easedale.
,, .	Moss Parrock .	—	Small open space in this village.
Hawkshead .	The Courthouse .	—	A picturesque pre-Reformation building.
Keld, near Shap	Keld Chapel. .	—	A small pre-Reformation building of the fifteenth or sixteenth century, about ten miles south of Penrith.
Keswick .	Druids' Circle .	9	A Bronze-Age circle of large stones, two miles from Keswick, near the old Penrith road.
Langdale .	Old Dungeon Ghyll Hotel, Stool End and Wall End Farms	400	Farm and fell lands at the dalehead (not all with public access).
Monk Coniston	Tarn Hows, Tom Gill, Yew Tree Farm, etc.	2770	A beautiful estate which joins up with the Duddon Valley properties and includes Holme Fell, Tilberthwaite Farm, and Wetherlam.

Locality.	Name of Property.	Approx. Acreage.	Remarks.
Rydal . .	Dora's Field . .	—	Originally bought by the poet Wordsworth in 1826, and given by his grandson.
,, . .	White Moss Intake	5½	Adjoins White Moss Common, near Grasmere. A rough pasture commanding fine view of Rydal Water.
Scafell . .	Scafell . . .	?	Adjoins Scafell Pike and the Fell and Rock Club Memorial property, and mostly above the 2000-ft. contour.
,, . .	Scafell Pike . .	?	Adjoins Scafell. The actual summit of the mountain (3210 ft.) down to the 3000-ft. contour.
Ullswater .	Glencoyne Wood .	180	Adjoins Stybarrow Crag, near Glenridding, and includes the lake shore.
,, .	Gowbarrow Fell .	750	Three miles from Glenridding; includes the waterfall Aira Force, and one mile of the lake shore. There is a herd of wild red deer on the fell.
Windermere .	Cockshott Point .	20	Includes the Rectory Farm at Bowness, and enjoys fine views of the lake.
,, .	Post Knott . .	7	A piece of rough land above Bowness with a good westerly view.

Locality.	Name of Property.	Approx. Acreage.	Remarks.
Windermere	Bordriggs Brow .	—	A view-point near Bowness, on the Crook road.
,, .	Queen Adelaide's Hill	20	On the lake side at Miller Ground, commanding splendid views.
,, .	Latterheath . .	40	Heathland on Moor How, two miles north of Windermere.
,, .	Allen Knott . .	—	View-point overlooking Troutbeck Valley and Lake Windermere.
,, .	Ladyholme . .	—	A small island and the site of an ancient chapel.

N.B.—In addition to the above-mentioned properties, the Trust has secured valuable protective covenants on other lands, notably at Buttermere, Derwentwater, Ullswater, Hawkshead and Nether Wasdale, covering roughly 6000 acres.

WORKING MEN'S COLLEGE
LIBRARY.

INDEX OF PLACE NAMES